D
13.2
W 74

DISCARD

The Writi
tory

D0425923

DATE DUE

T 2064

THE WRITING OF HISTORY

D
13.2
W74

8096

The Writing of HISTORY

Literary Form and Historical Understanding

Edited by

ROBERT H. CANARY

and

HENRY KOZICKI

The University of Wisconsin Press

Published 1978
The University of Wisconsin Press
Box 1379, Madison, Wisconsin 53701

The University of Wisconsin Press, Ltd.
70 Great Russell Street, London

Copyright © 1978
The Board of Regents of the University of Wisconsin System
All Rights Reserved

First Printing

Printed in the United States of America

For LC CIP information see the colophon

ISBN 0-299-07570-2

Contributors

KIERAN EGAN
Faculty of Education
Simon Fraser University
Burnaby, British Columbia

LIONEL GOSSMAN
Department of Romance Languages and Literatures
Princeton University
Princeton, New Jersey

LOUIS O. MINK
Department of Philosophy
Wesleyan University
Middletown, Connecticut

RICHARD REINITZ
Department of History
Hobart and William Smith Colleges
Geneva, New York

HAYDEN WHITE
The Center for the Humanities
Wesleyan University
Middletown, Connecticut

CONTENTS

INTRODUCTION

The five essays in this volume deal with the relationship between the content of historical writing and the literary form in which it is presented. Two of the authors are historians, two are literary critics, and one is a philosopher. Each brings his own point of view from his own discipline to illuminate a particular aspect of the larger subject.

The intellectual task of determining the relationship between historical narratives and other narrative forms dates back at least to Aristotle. Lionel Gossman sketches the history of that intellectual enterprise in the opening essay, and the other authors address in different ways the theoretical bases of the relationship. All are in general agreement on three propositions: that the historian's use of narrative directly influences the extent to which he conveys an accurate and intelligible understanding of the past, that historical narrative raises problems for the philosopher concerned with the nature of historical knowledge, and that this literary form provides an opportunity for the literary critic to gauge the aesthetic dimensions of writings whose literary appeal has or will be proven more lasting than their standing as definitive history. At least some of the contributors share our belief that histories which are not written in the narrative mode are also literary products, but that is another subject. The statements we have just made define a fairly certain consensus in regard to historical narrative.

We leave to the contributors the task of arguing the points we have outlined above. Our task in this Introduction is to justify the existence of a volume composed of such essays. One might think that an intellectual enterprise of such respectable antiquity and such obvious intellectual interest to several academic disciplines would require no special presentation and defense. We think it does. We believe that the literary and aesthetic qualities of historical writing have been given too little attention by historians, philosophers, and literary critics, particularly in America. Moreover, we believe that valuable work being done in one discipline or another on this topic is too little known outside of that discipline.

The neglect of which we complain is not a matter of historical accident but a by-product of the organization of knowledge into professionalized specialties. Specialization of this sort is quite possibly inevitable given the principles that govern division of labor in an industrial society and quite certainly useful given the great increase in historical, scientific, and other knowledge at our disposal. Our own interdisciplinary commitments do not require us to hark back to some supposed Golden Age of philosopher kings or to anticipate an interdisciplinary revolution in which the academic department and specialized journal will wither away. But resignation to the inevitability and even utility of disciplinary specialization does not entail approval of all of its consequences. The neglect of relevant issues because they are thought safely assigned to some other discipline is one unhappy consequence of the disciplinary organization of knowledge. We believe that the essays in this volume show that the proper relationship between history and other forms of literature is not one of the issues that can safely be assigned to any one discipline.

Historians are already familiar with the general form of this sort of criticism. Let us say that our historian has spent four years mastering the materials for a dissertation on the politics of Populism in Tennessee and is wondering how to find time to work in the archives of other Border States. Colleagues urge the necessity of mastering statistical theory, to analyze voting patterns, and Russian, to use the work of Soviet historians. To understand the complex economic issues involved, our historian is urged to become something of an economist; to understand the complex personalities involved, psychohistorians recommend a year in analysis. Listening to such exhortations at scholarly conventions refreshes him as the Sunday sermon on the evil of riches refreshes the banker, giving our historian strength to return to work on his purely political history of Populism in the Border States.

Our historian need not worry, however. We do not propose to ask him to become a literary critic or a philosopher but to persuade him that he is already a litterateur and may thus have something to learn from the observations of literary critics and philosophers about the nature of historical narrative. Deliberate restriction of research aims may enable the historian to evade with good conscience the demands of one external discipline or another, but when he sets out to tell the story of what he has learned from his research he has committed himself to language and to form. We would argue that he will make literary choices at every turn and should make them consciously. Language is as much a part of his materials as his research data, and command of his materials is the mark of a good historian.

Although the essays that follow are intended to be of interest even to the historian of Border State Populism, they are obviously more directly relevant to the historiographer. There is, of course, more than one kind of historiography. Besides the history of historical writing, the term is also used to refer to studies in the methodology of historical writing. Despite the existence of some distinguished exceptions, it seems only fair to say that American historians have in general been less sophisticated than their European confreres in their approach to both kinds of historiography. In writing the history of history, they have often focused on the personal lives and interpretative disputes of historians at the expense of the larger context of intellectual history and the history of the professions. In discussions of methodology, they have often focused on research tools—a "cookbook" approach. In each case, the literary qualities of historical works are touched on briefly, if at all, and are rarely accorded much significance.

The narrow focus of so much historiography in America is probably another result of the high degree of specialization and professionalization of history in America. The neglect of literary dimensions may have an additional cause in the observable tendency of American historians to equate "literature" in history with style. When pursued by a master, as in Peter Gay's *Style in History,* an interest in style may lead one to significant issues. But when style is conceived of as mere decoration, sugarcoating on the historical substance, considerations of history as literature naturally seem of little moment to the historian. Such a conception is, in fact, a rather naîve view of the relationship between a message and its medium. In any case, style is not the only, and probably not the primary, literary quality relevant to our consideration of historical works. Aristotle, at least, thought plot more important than style in literature, and the choice of total narrative form would certainly seem more important in history, for the pattern of the narrative is itself an interpretative statement. The essays that follow are all concerned with matters larger than style.

Having painted this barren picture of American historiography, let us admit that we believe that the present crisis in the historical profession is encouraging a self-consciousness which should produce a more sophisticated historiography, though one hardly wants to see advances depend on there being large numbers of unemployed historians. For whatever reason, a historiography more closely linked to intellectual history is already at hand in the work of men like Georg Iggers and Gene Wise, while Robert Berkhofer has given us a model of a more sophisticated consideration of methodological opportunities. For those interested in the relationship between literature and history, the key work is probably Hayden White's *Metahistory*, which is also an important contribution to our reflections on nineteenth-century European intellectual history. Although widely reviewed, White's work does not seem to us to have yet had the degree of impact it should, especially among historians of other periods and areas. Even sympathetic reviewers expressed some resistance to the literary analysis employed in that work, a resistance not merely to his conclusions, which are certainly open to debate, but to his very methods. Relatively few literary critics, outside of, say, Michelet scholars, seem to have read *Metahistory*. The essay by White in this volume gives the reader an idea of the direction of White's thought, and the essay by Reinitz shows that White is not alone among current historians in pursuing such interests.

The modern separation of history and literature is paralleled by a separation of history and philosophy. Too few historiographers in the Anglo-American tradition seem to have paid serious attention to contemporary philosophy of history, even when debating such obviously philosophical questions as what a historical fact might be or what the nature and purpose of history as a branch of knowledge is or should be, though White is, again, one of the exceptions. In many ways, this indifference is reciprocated, as one can verify by noting how few American philosophers list the philosophy of history as a major interest or, more subjectively, how ahistorical most work in the "history of philosophy" seems when compared, say, to the history of science. One must admit, of course, that the philosophy of history is logically dependent upon more basic questions in epistemology, but the consequences of disciplinary specialization may also play a part. Anglo-American philosophy has often come to seem a philosophy of the right ways to carry on philosophical discourse, and it may be not entirely accidental that the most lively issues in philosophy of history for the past quarter-century have been in the area of discourse—in particular, one thinks of the great debate over the nature of historical explanation. Since such debates often revolve around efforts to subsume historical explanation under some more inclusive rubric, history naturally assumes a less central role than it did in the nineteenth century, when questions about the meaning of history were more generally agreed to be in order. But though one may feel that some major historical problems have been slighted, it is certainly the case that contemporary philosophy has led to insights into the nature of historical narrative and narrative generally. We believe that both historiographers and literary critics concerned with narrative could benefit from some acquaintance with contemporary philosophy of history. Those most obviously relevant to our present purpose are the philosophers willing to take seriously the possibility that narrative, as employed by historians, may constitute a distinct and defensible form of explanation. We believe that the essay by Louis Mink in this volume demonstrates the relevance and utility of such analyses.

The problems of specialization in literature resemble those in history, intensified by the sheer numbers in a field like English and by the terrible facility with which an ambitious literary critic can publish, unhampered by the historian's need to do archival research between books and articles. For the student of historical literature, there are additional complicating factors. First, the dominant critical school in America has approached literature with methods best geared to poetry. One may link this to specialization if one assumes that lyric poetry (and even epic poetry is often treated as if it were lyric in mode) represents an essential "literariness," being the most dependent of literary forms on language itself, the least on social context; this may fit with the low status often assigned to social novels. Whatever the source of this preoccupation with diction and symbol, it little fits critics for consideration of historical writing. A second factor is harder to explain: though in practice literary scholarship seems increasingly critical, even to the point of being ahistorical, the organization of literary scholarship still reflects the days when literary history was dominant, so that practitioners are apt to identify themselves with periods and areas. The training of American literary critics remains broad enough that new lines of approach to favored forms are transmitted relatively quickly within the profession, but there is less communication of methodologies applied to the relatively neglected forms, which are not part of the standard curriculum.

There are, in fact, a good number of literary critics working on historical literature. Whatever critical consensus there has been is breaking up; narrative is back in favor; many are deliberately trying to revive a broader conception of "literature." What one does not sense, as yet, is any clear feeling of common concern among those working in the genre. Leo Braudy's admirable *Narrative Form in History and Fiction: Hume, Fielding, and Gibbon* needs to be placed on the same shelf with David Levin's equally admirable *History as Romantic Art*, which deals with the American historians Bancroft, Prescott, Motley, and Parkman. There are still too few such works, and it is wasteful to allow them to be pigeonholed in the minor category of "works concerned with the nonfiction prose of the period." Historiographers, too, of whatever period, could also benefit from such works as models. It is bad enough that one can still encounter essays on Parkman, for example, which do not mention the work of either Levin or his student, Richard Vitzthum. But a historiographer of any period could learn from Levin something of how one may deal with matters like the presentation of historical characters. The general issues raised by any literary critic's treatment of historical writing are taken up in this volume by Lionel Gossman, and Kieran Egan's essay demonstrates one form such investigations may take.

The authors of the essays in this book do not constitute a distinct "school," though four of them have some connection with the journal *Clio*. The disciplinary fragmentation we have complained of virtually precludes the existence of some solid phalanx of historiographers, literary critics, and philosophers dedicated to advancing the banners of history as literature. Even the editors' polemical intent does not go so far as to seek to create such a phalanx. The essays represent efforts still often seen as marginal in their own disciplines and still little known in other disciplines. Our hope is that bringing together examples of this work will help the reader see the work being done in any one area in a new light, as part of a more general advance taking place in several disciplines at the same time.

In arranging the essays for this volume, we have placed first the essays by Lionel Gossman and Hayden White. Gossman's essay provides a useful historical perspective and an introduction to the literary and historical issues raised by the authors who follow. White's essay sharpens the issues and provides a programmatic statement. The authors, a literary critic and historian respectively, share a common scholarly interest in Michelet. As their essays demonstrate, approaching the same problem from different disciplinary backgrounds has not kept them from achieving a certain measure of agreement on basic issues. Our next two essays, by Kieran Egan and Richard Reinitz, can be seen in many ways as carrying out the kind of program implied by the two theoretical essays. Again we find two scholars from different disciplinary backgrounds applying similar methods of analysis, in Egan's analysis of the tragic elements in Thucydides and in Reinitz's analysis of the ironic mode in four American historians. Our final essay, by Louis Mink, again returns us to the theoretical plane, with a philosopher's assessment of the assumptions underlying the use of narrative form. We believe his observations gain critical point from following the efforts of Egan and Reinitz. We hope that the reader will want to pursue the questions raised in these essays; for this reason we have appended a brief bibliographical essay. We hope, too, that the reader will find that these essays affect the way he thinks about history and historical writing, and that some readers will want to join the authors herein in investigating the literary structures that help shape historical writing.

ROBERT H. CANARY   HENRY KOZICKI
University of Wisconsin–Parkside   *Indiana University–*
Kenosha, Wisconsin   *Purdue University*
                                                            Fort Wayne, Indiana

December 1977

THE WRITING OF HISTORY

Lionel Gossman

1
HISTORY AND
LITERATURE
Reproduction or Signification

> Le problème essentiel est de savoir si l'objet est
> signifié ou reconstitué ou, du moins, lequel des
> deux buts on se propose d'atteindre puisqu'en
> fait, on ne reconstitue jamais l'objet.
>
> Claude Lévi-Strauss,
> in Georges Charbonnier,
> *Entretiens avec Claude Lévi-Strauss*

For a long time the relation of history to literature was not notably
problematic. History was a branch of literature. It was not until the
meaning of the word literature, or the institution of literature itself,
began to change, toward the end of the eighteenth century, that history came to appear as something distinct from literature.

Quintilian treats history as a form of epic. Of all prose forms, it is
the closest to poetry—a kind of prose poem: "Est enim proxima
poetis et quodam modo carmen solutum est et scribitur ad narrandum
non ad probandum."[1] Because his object is not to demonstrate or
argue or persuade, but to narrate and to memorialize, according to
Quintilian, the historian may properly employ unfamiliar expressions
and bold figures that would be out of place and ineffective in forensic
rhetoric. The brief discussion of particular historians in the *Institutio*
deals almost exclusively with the stylistic features of their work. Cicero also distinguishes between the mere chronicling of events *sine
ullis ornamentis,* such as was practiced by the earliest Roman annal-
ists, and the literary productions of the Greek historians. Like Quintilian, he emphasizes that the rhetoric of history is not part of forensic
rhetoric—few of the Greek historians, he claims, had any experience
of pleading in a court of law—and he complains that no rhetorician
has yet formulated the principles of historical writing.[2]

Cicero's own tentative formulation of the basic principles of a future rhetoric of history—the historian may say nothing false, he must

1. *Institutio oratoria* X. 1. 31.
2. *De oratore* II. 51–64.

3

dare to say all that is true, he must avoid partiality—seems to remove the question of history from the province of rhetoric to that of episte- mology. In fact, Cicero does not neglect matters of style and presen- tation. He merely questions the relevance of forensic rhetoric to the writing of history. And his conception of the historian as the imper- sonal mirror of reality is entirely consistent with traditional philoso- phy and aesthetics. It is repeated, moreover, by other classical writers who concerned themselves with history: Tacitus, Polybius, Plutarch, Lucian. "The ancients' theory of history," it has been said, "was limited largely to questions of technique and presentation."[3]

Renaissance reflection on historiography conformed, as one would expect, to the precepts of the ancients. History writing was viewed as an art of presentation rather than a scientific inquiry, and its problems belonged therefore to rhetoric rather than to epistemology. Though seventeenth- and eighteenth-century theories of poetry usually left room for a neo-Platonic notion of divine inspiration inherited from the Renaissance, literature had, for the most part, the sense of a practice, a technique. A person "of considerable . . . literature" (Mary Edge- worth, 1802, quoted in *OED,* s.v. "literature") was someone who had a considerable repertory of the models by which a good craftsman should be guided, not only in his judgments of the work of others but in his own activity. Speaking of France, Sartre observes that the gap between writer and reader in the seventeenth century was not great. Every reader was himself, in a lesser way, a writer.[4] "Literature" thus referred to the practice of writing. And history—along with ser- mons, eulogies, and letters—was one of the kinds of writing that could be practiced. The subjects varied and required different treat- ment, but the craft was the same.[5] History thus had its place in manuals of rhetoric throughout the eighteenth century. It was always

3. Rudolf Unger, "Zur Entwicklung des Problems der historischen Objektivität bis Hegel," orig. pub. in *Aufsätze zur Prinzipienlehre der Literaturgeschichte* (Berlin, 1929), trans. as "The Problem of Historical Objectivity: A Sketch of Its Development to the Time of Hegel," in *Enlightenment Historiography: Three German Studies* (*His- tory and Theory: Studies in the Philosophy of History,* Beiheft 11, Middletown, Conn.: Wesleyan Univ. Press, 1971), p. 63.

4. Jean-Paul Sartre, *Qu'est-ce que la littérature?* (1948; rpt. Paris: Gallimard, 1964), pp. 112–13.

5. See Hugh Blair, *Lectures on Rhetoric and Belles Lettres* (London: W. Strahan and T. Cadell, 1783), 2:274 (Lecture 36): "But an Historian may possess these qualities of being perspicuous, distinct, and grave, and may notwithstanding be a dull Writer; in which case, we shall reap little benefit from his labours. We will read him without pleasure; or, most probably, we shall soon give over to read him at all. He must therefore study to render his narration interesting; which is the quality that chiefly distinguishes a Writer of genius and eloquence."

distinguishable from "mere" scholarship and antiquarianism, and the ground of the distinction was in large measure that the historian was a writer, whereas the scholar and the antiquarian were not. Gibbon expressed a common view when he wrote that histories become of less and less interest to readers as the events of which they tell become more remote. They come, indeed, to lose "presque tout leur mérite, excepté celui que leur auteur a su leur donner par la manière dont il a traité son sujet."[6] Rudolf Unger's characterization of historiography in the classical period—"historiography was accounted to be, in the first instance, a *literary* genre"[7]—remains valid for the practice of history until nearly the end of the eighteenth century.

In the final phase of neoclassicism, however, the long association of rhetoric and literature began to break down. The term "literature" gradually became more closely associated with poetry, or at least with poetic and figurative writing, and, especially among the Romantics and their successors, took on the meaning of a corpus of privileged or sacred texts, a treasury in which value, truth, and beauty had been piously stored, and which could be opposed to the empirical world of historical reality and even, to some extent, to historiography as the faithful record of that reality. Indeed, it was at this point that historians began to look in the history of historiography itself for the origins of a divorce—which they felt their own time was about to consummate—between historical writing and poetic writing. In the article "History," which he wrote for the *Encyclopédie moderne,* Prosper de Barante located in ancient Greece, just before Herodotus, the fatal moment when "the real was separated from the ideal, poetry from prose, the pleasures men allow themselves in the domain of the spirit from the positive aspects of life."[8] The new conception of literature was more appropriate than the earlier, artisanal one to the condition of the writer in the age of the triumphant bourgeoisie and of industrial capitalism, marking both a criticism of these and a complicity with them. It allowed the products of art to appear as essentially different from all other products of labor in the degraded world of industry and the market, but in order to do so, it foregrounded, in-

6. "Remarques sur les ouvrages et sur le caractère de Salluste, Jules César, Cornelius Nepos, et Tite-Live," *Miscellaneous Works* (London: J. Murray, 1814), 4:430–31. Similar comments by Voltaire in a "Discours sur *l'Histoire de Charles XII*" appended to the early editions of this work.

7. "Problem of Historical Objectivity," p. 73. Cf. Prosper de Barante's judgment of seventeenth-century historiography: "L'art historique doit maintenant être considéré comme une branche de la littérature" ("De l'histoire," in *Mélanges historiques et littéraires* [Brussels: J. P. Méline, 1835], 2:34).

8. Barante, "De l'histoire," p. 8.

deed fetishized, the product, concealing or mystifying the processes of its production. Literature thus ceased to be thought of as an art by which ideas could be conveyed effectively and elegantly, and which could be pursued with varying degrees of skill and success by all educated people. More and more it came to be regarded as a magical or religious mission, which only those endowed with the gift of prophecy or second sight could fulfil.

Most recently, throwing off in turn the mantle of prophecy, writers have sought to emancipate literature from the myth of Literature, and to turn it into a self-conscious tool for exploring language and extending its range—that is to say, the range of social perception and meaning. Instead of simply accepting language, together with the secondary categories of literary norms and genres, as given, and working within the conditions it provides, the modern writer is constantly crossing frontiers and extending outward the limits and possibilities of writing. The focus of the literary artist's activity, in short, has shifted from rhetoric to poetics. The writer is now not so much a revealer of truths, a speaker of divine language, as a maker of meanings and a restorer of human languages.

At the same time that literature began to detach itself from rhetoric, history was also altering the focus of its concern. For the first time, the epistemological basis of its ideal of impartially copying or representing the real was put in question. As early as 1752, the German theologian Johann Martin Chladenius, elaborating a position outlined by Leibniz and Bayle, made the concept of point of view fundamental to all historical narrative.

> We cannot avoid that each of us looks on the story according to his point of view and that therefore we also retell it according to that point of view . . . . A narration wholly abstracted from its own point of view is impossible, and hence an impartial narration cannot be called one that narrates without any point of view at all, for such simply is not possible. Likewise to be biased in the telling cannot be equated with narrating a subject or a story from one's point of view, for if that were the case all narrations would be biased."

Though Chladenius himself resolved the difficulty too neatly, suggesting that a combination of points of view would allow the object to be located and perceived "objectively," subsequent reflection on historiography, particularly in Germany, was overwhelmingly preoccupied

9. *Allgemeine Geschichtswissenschaft worinnen der Grund zu einer neuen Einsicht in allen Arten der Gelehrtheit gelegt wird* (Leipzig, 1752), pp. 150–52, quoted in Unger, "Problem of Historical Objectivity," p. 71.

with discovering a more comprehensive theory of historical objectivity than naïve realism, one that would include and subsume subjectivity. Despite their differences, Humboldt, Savigny, Ranke, Creuzer, Schleiermacher, Gervinus, and Hegel were all concerned with this problem. Their speculation led to a conception of historical knowledge that emphasized its peculiarity with respect to the knowledge provided by the natural sciences. Positivist theories of history, on the other hand, aimed to bring history as close as possible, epistemologically and methodologically, to the natural sciences. Reflection on historiography was thus more and more concerned with the problems of historical knowledge, and very rarely, or only incidentally, with the problems of historical writing. The separation of literature and historiography was institutionalized, moreover, by the breakup of what had once been the republic of letters—a society in which the historians, both of the Enlightenment and of the early Romantic period, especially in France, England, and Scotland, had mingled freely and shared common experiences and aspirations with novelists, poets, philosophers, political thinkers, economists, scientists, and statesmen. In the course of the nineteenth century, historians withdrew more and more to the university, to be followed by historians of literature and by literary critics, and history, like literary scholarship, passed from the hands of the poet and man of letters into those of the professor. Finally, in our own times, the very idea that the historian's activity consists in discovering and reconstituting, by whatever means, a past reality conceived of as something objectively fixed, has begun to be questioned. The old common ground of history and literature—the idea of mimesis, and the central importance of rhetoric—has thus been gradually vacated by both. The practicing historian is now rarely a practicing literary artist, and the long road traveled by Herodotus, Sallust, Livy, Plutarch, Voltaire, Gibbon, Macaulay, and Michelet appears finally to have been abandoned by all but a handful of stragglers.

Over a long period of time, then, it seems that the terms whose relations we have to explore are not so much literature and history—since these were not exclusive—as fictional narrative ("fictional history," as Hugh Blair called it) and historical narrative, that is to say, the two terms whose relation has traditionally been of concern to rhetoricians. I would like to comment briefly on this relation, which was a productive one for both fiction and history, before broaching the question of the relation of history and literature in a more recent context.

The traditional outline of the relation was traced by Aristotle in two famous passages of the *Poetics*.

> A poetic imitation, then, ought to be unified in the same way as a single imitation in any other mimetic field, by having a single object: since the plot is an imitation of an action, the latter ought to be both unified and complete, and the component events ought to be so firmly compacted that if any one of them is shifted to another place, or removed, the whole is loosened up and dislocated; for an element whose addition or subtraction makes no perceptible extra difference is not really a part of the whole.
>
> From what has been said it is also clear that the poet's job is not to report what has happened but what is likely to happen: that is, what is capable of happening according to the rule of probability or necessity. Thus the difference between the historian and the poet is not in their utterances being in verse or prose (it would be quite possible for Herodotus' work to be translated into verse, and it would not be any the less a history with verse than it is without it); the difference lies in the fact that the historian speaks of what has happened, the poet of the kind of thing that *can* happen. Hence also poetry is a more philosophical and serious business than history; for poetry speaks more of universals, history of particulars. "Universal" in this case is what kind of person is likely to do or say certain kinds of things, according to probability or necessity; that is what poetry aims at, although it gives its persons particular names afterward; while the "particular" is what Alcibiades did or what happened to him. [51a30–51b13]
>
> It is clear that epic plots should be made dramatic, as in tragedies, dealing with a single action that is whole and complete and has beginning, middles, and end, so that like a single complete creature it may produce the appropriate pleasure. It is also clear that the plot-structure should not resemble a history, in which of necessity a report is presented not of a single action but of a single period, including everything that happened during that time to individuals or groups—of which events each has only chance relationships to the others. For just as the sea battle at Salamis and the battle against the Carthaginians in Sicily took place about the same time of year but in no way pointed toward the same goal, so also in successive periods spread over time it often happens that one event follows another without any single result coming from them. Yet, speaking by and large, most poets compose this way.
>
> That is why, in addition to what has been said about him previously, one can hardly avoid feeling that Homer showed god-like genius in this case also, namely in the fact that although the Trojan War had a beginning and an end, he did not undertake to compose it as a whole either. For the plot would have been bound to turn out too long and not easy

to encompass in a glance, or, if it held to some measurable length, to become entangled with the diversity of its events. Instead, he has singled out one part of the whole and used many of the others as episodes . . . . [59a20–59a37][10]

Aristotle thus defines history and poetry, in typically classical manner, antithetically: poetry is unified, intelligible, based on proper subordination of the part to the ends of the whole, whereas history knows only the paratactic organization of contiguity or succession. "Aristotle took a low view of history," D. W. Lucas writes in his recent edition of the *Poetics*. "It contains a mere congeries of events, either those of a short period, which will belong to numerous different πϱάξεις [actions], or those of a longer period, which will again tend to no one τέλος [end]. As Aristotle nowhere censures the historian he must have thought that the complexity of events combined with deficiency of information made it impossible to disentangle the underlying relationships. . . . The point is that history, not being concerned with πϱάξεις, is not intelligible in the same way as the μῦθος [plot] of a play."[11] The distinction, in short, is in some measure, at least, formal, and the operative characteristic of the

10. Quoted from the translation by Gerald F. Else (Ann Arbor: Univ. of Michigan Press, 1967). Hegel's distinction between history and poetry in *The Philosophy of Fine Art* (Part III, subsection iii, chapter III, subsection 2) marks a considerable modification of Aristotle's distinction between history and epic, but the framework in which it is made remains strikingly similar: "The historian . . . has no right to expunge these prosaic characteristics of his content, or to convert them into others more *poetical;* his narrative must embrace what lies actually before him and in the shape he finds it without amplification, or at least poetical transformation. However much, therefore, it may become a part of his labours to make the ideal significance and spirit of an epoch, a people, or the particular event depicted, the ideal focus and bond which holds all together in one coherent whole, he is not entitled to make either the conditions presented him, the characters or events, wholly subordinate to such a purpose, though he may doubtless remove from his survey what is wholly contingent and without serious significance: he must, in short, permit them to appear in all their objective contingency, dependence and mysterious caprice. . . . And, finally, if the historian adds to his survey his private reflections as a philosopher, attempting thereby to grasp the absolute grounds for such events, rising to the sphere of that divine being, before which all that is contingent vanishes and a loftier mode of necessity is unveiled, he is nonetheless debarred, in reference to the actual conformation of events, from that exclusive right of poetry, namely to accept this substantive resolution as the fact of most importance. To poetry alone is the liberty permitted to dispose without restriction of the material submitted in such a way that it becomes, even regarded on the side of external condition, conformable with ideal truth" (quoted from the translation by F. P. B. Osmaston [London: G. Bell, 1920], 4:41–42).

11. Oxford: Clarendon, 1968, p. 119.

μῦθος is not apparently whether it is fact or fiction, as we would say, but its unity or unifying power.[12]

Traditionally, then, history and fictional story-telling confront and challenge each other at opposite poles of narrative practice. The actual development of each, however, reveals both great similarities and some significant tensions. Since each is realized in and through narrative, the shape of narrative and the view of the world that particular narrative forms convey may well be common to both at any given time. In some periods, both will be constructed according to a principle of accumulation, association, or addition—vividly described by Albert Thibaudet's term *lopinisme*—in others, such as the neoclassical period, both will strive to conform to ideals of order, coherency, and hierarchical structure. But the tension between the requirements of system and those of change, between order and adventure, will usually persist in all kinds of narrative practice (historical or fictional) and may at certain moments become acute enough to become themselves the principal theme of narrative works. At such times, history may come to be associated, as it was in the *Poetics,* with the singular, the unexpected, the uncontrollable, the unsystematic, and fiction, on the other hand, with the ordered, the coherent, the general or universal. We may then discover that while historians are striving to achieve maximum narrative coherency and to approximate to the forms of fiction, certain novelists are trying to undercut these very forms and conventions by an appeal to "history."

As one of the founding fathers of modern historiography, Voltaire was much concerned with matters of form, and his lifelong reflection on historiography began, characteristically, as reflection on epic. In the early *Essay on Epick Poetry* (1727) he emphasized, conventionally enough, the exemplary character of the epic action and its unity. At the same time, he declared that he preferred the subject to be "true," and he criticized Le Bossu for advocating that the epic poet invent subjects out of his imagination. Virgil was said to have gathered together for the

12. Georg Simmel's interesting essay on "the adventure" (*Gesammelte Essays* [1911; 2nd enl. ed., Leipzig, 1919]), illuminates Aristotle's idea of the action. Simmel argues that the adventure constitutes a unity in itself, an episode that is discontinuous with the normal flow of our lives, yet "somehow connected with the center. . . . It is because the work of art and the adventure stand over against life . . . that both are analogous to the totality of life itself . . . .In contrast to those aspects of life which are related only peripherally—by mere fate—the adventure is defined by its capacity, in spite of its being isolated and accidental, to have necessity and meaning" (trans. David Rettler, in *Georg Simmel, 1858–1918*, ed. Kurt H. Wolff [Columbus: Ohio State Univ. Press, 1959], pp. 243–58).

Aeneid "different materials which were scattered through several books and of which some can be found in Dionysius Halicarnassiensis."[13] Virgil's materials, in sum, were basically "true." The notion of "true" here, however, is one that has become strange to us. Essentially, Voltaire means "familiar," "legendary," or "held to be true." The idea is hard to convey now, since the legendary has come to be synonymous with false. The important thing for Voltaire, on the other hand, in this context at any rate, was not objective truth, as distinct from subjective belief, but the fact that the material was part of a widely accepted tradition. For this very reason, he held that the modern writer should remove from traditional material all elements that might run counter to what his own readers would consider true, anything they might find unacceptable or "improbable." In short, the material best suited to the epic writer is that which has already been selected, filtered, and shaped by literary tradition and popular imagination, and which the epic writer in turn filters with his own audience in view, and preferably such material should be regarded by the public as generally "true." Recent history, which has not yet been worked over and given shape, is too raw to serve successfully. With much sympathy for Lucan, Voltaire attributes what he considered the failure of the *Pharsalia* to the recalcitrance of the material, and he makes a similar point somewhat later in a comment on his own epic poem *La Henriade* (1728): "This poem is based on a known history, the truth of which has been respected in the principal events. The others, being less reliable, have been either omitted or rearranged according to the requirements of verisimilitude ("vraisemblance") in a poetic composition. In this way, every effort has been made to avoid the weakness of Lucan, whose poem is nothing but an overblown chronicle."[14] Lucan is compared favorably with Tasso, however, because the latter invented his subject.

Voltaire's alternatives in this early essay are clearly those of the *Poetics:* the pure succession of history and the formal unity of legend. The "truth" he requires of the epic narrative is not yet defined against legend or myth. Yet in his own first attempt at epic composi-

13. Translated from Voltaire's French version of the *Essay* (1733), *Oeuvres complètes,* ed. Louis Moland, 52 vols. (Paris: Garnier Frères, 1877–85), 8:322. (All translations are mine unless otherwise indicated.) Cf. Addison, *Spectator,* 2:520: "The Reader may find an abridgement of the whole Story as collected out of the ancient Historians, and as it was received among the Romans, in *Dionysius Halicarnasseus.*" The original English text of Voltaire's *Essay* says only: "Part of the Events included in the *Aeneid* are to be found in *Dionysius Halicarnassus*" (*Voltaire's Essay on Epic Poetry: A Study and an Edition,* ed. Florence D. White [Albany, N. Y.: Brandow, 1915], p. 94).

14. "Idée de la Henriade," *Oeuvres,* 8:39.

tion—roughly contemporary with the *Essay*—Voltaire shows the influence of the demand for criticism and verification which corresponded, in the scholarly circles of the seventeenth century, to the austere standards of the new philosophy and its obsession with falsehood and error. The notion of the "true" in the *Henriade* is already close to that of modern historical "science." The *Henriade* was always regarded by both the author and his readers as a work of history; and both considered that, as such, it had to meet the standards of the new historical criticism. It was not enough simply to work over familiar material widely held to be true. The material had to be authenticated, the subject shown to be true. Early editions of the text were accompanied by an "Histoire abrégée des événements historiques sur lesquels est fondée la fable du poème de la Henriade." A "Dissertation sur la mort de Henri IV" was added by Voltaire himself to the 1748 edition, and the Kehl editors appended further documentary evidence, as well as a translation into French of the "Essay on the Civil Wars in France," which had accompanied the first edition of the *Essay on Epick Poetry*. In the late nineteenth century Louis Moland still gave serious consideration to the historical value of the work.

The demands of historical criticism affected content alone, however. They imposed new constraints and obligations on the historian in the selection of the material he proposed to work over, but did not alter the fundamental fact that his task was to *write,* to compose a coherent work of literature with data provided by history. The "Essay on the Civil Wars" and the "Histoire abrégée" are revealing in this respect. Doubtless they were to be understood as the unadorned version, the bare bones of the literary work. Each canto, moreover, opened with a brief prose summary of the events or the theme to be amplified in verse in it, a tactic that Voltaire continued in his later prose histories and that was traditionally followed by writers of romances and writers of histories alike. The difference between the historian and the epic poet, for Voltaire, thus lay in the nature of the material out of which each composed his work. In the conditions of modern critical thought the material of the one could no longer be identical with that of the other. Historical material and legendary material were now distinct. Nevertheless, the essential concerns of the epic poet and of the historian, not as scholar but as writer, were the same: careful selection of an appropriate subject matter, and skillful narrative composition. Voltaire's discussions not only of the *Henriade,* but of the *Histoire de Charles XII* and the *Siècle de Louis XIV* leave no doubt about this; the comments of his correspondents—especially of those who wrote to him about the *Histoire de Charles*

XII—make it abundantly clear that readers, on their side, judged historical narrative according to the criteria applied to fictional narrative. "L'histoire," in Cideville's pithy phrase, "n'est qu'un plus long conte."[15] Voltaire, in short, preferred his epics to be true and his histories to be epic. Indeed, it is possible to view his historiographical career as the continuation of a career begun in the practice of epic. When he wrote to Hénault about the design of the *Siècle de Louis XIV* he probably still had Aristotle's observations on history and epic in mind.

> My aim has been to make a great picture of events that are worthy of being painted, and to keep the reader's eyes trained on the leading characters. History, like tragedy, requires an exposition, a central action, and a denouement. Otherwise the historian is no more than a Reboulet, or a Limiers, or a La Hode. There is room, moreover, in this vast canvas for interesting anecdotes. I hate petty facts; plenty of others have laden their enormous compilations with them . . . . My secret is to force the reader to wonder: Will Philip V ascend the throne? Will he be chased out of Spain? Will Holland be destroyed? Will Louis XIV go under? In short, I have tried to move my reader, even in history.[16]

Voltaire was not alone in wishing to make history the modern successor of the epic. Gibbon's essay on "Mr. Hurd's Commentary on Horace" (1757) shows how much thought he gave to questions of epic composition, and the narrator of the *Decline and Fall* accompanies his narrative with a continuous commentary on its composition.[17] As is well known, Gibbon considered a number of topics before finally selecting the decline and fall of the Roman Empire as the subject of his great history. His principal concern was the appropriateness of the

15. Letter to Voltaire, March 17, 1757, in *Voltaire's Correspondence*, ed. T. Besterman, 107 vols. (Geneva: Institut et Musée Voltaire, 1956–65), No. 6507.

16. Ibid., letter of August 1, 1752 (No. 4163). These comments on the later prose history were anticipated by an earlier comment on the *Henriade:* "All nations are agreed that a simple unified action, developed gradually and without being forced, . . . is more pleasing than a chaotic pile of monstrous adventures. In general, there is a desire that this reasonable unity be ornamented by a variety of episodes which will be like the limbs of a robust and well-proportioned body" (*Oeuvres*, 8:308–9).

17. E.g., Chapter 11: "We might distribute into three acts this remarkable tragedy"; Chapter 34: "I am not desirous to prolong or repeat this narration"; Chapter 43: "Should I persevere in the same course, should I observe the same measure, a prolix and slender thread would be spun through many a volume, nor would the patient reader find an adequate reward of instruction or amusement." In general, Gibbon holds, the "scope of narrative, the riches and variety of . . . materials" should not "be incompatible with the unity of design and composition" (Chapter 48).

subject matter to the kind of literary treatment he had in mind. In his *Lettre sur les occupations de l'Académie* (1716) Fénelon had already urged a reform of the manner of writing history that would have given to history the status and the form of epic. "A dry and dreary compiler of annals knows no other order than that of chronology. . . . But the historian of genius selects among twenty possible places in his narrative the one where a fact ought to be placed to throw light on all the others."[18] Aristotle notwithstanding, in other words, the historian ought to be concerned with "actions" and ought to organize his material accordingly. Instead of a pure succession, a genealogy, he should recount an action that has an exposition, a central intrigue, and a denouement, and that illustrates some important principle.

Later in the century, Hugh Blair's teaching in his rhetoric classes at the University of Edinburgh was similar. "Historical composition is understood to comprehend under it, Annals, Memoirs, Lives," Blair allowed. "But these," he added, "are its inferior subordinate species. In the conduct and management of his subject, the first attention requisite in an Historian is to give as much unity as possible; that is, his History should not consist of separate unconnected parts merely, but should be bound together by some connecting principle, which shall make the impression on the mind of something that is one, whole and entire." The reader is most pleased and instructed "when the mind has always before it the progress of some one great plan or system of actions; when there is some point or centre, to which we can refer the various facts related by the Historian."[19] Just as Montesquieu claimed that in the *Lettres persanes* he had joined philosophy, politics, and morals to a novel, and bound them into a unified composition by "une chaîne secrète," Blair argued that in history "we should be able to trace all the secret links of the chain, which binds together remote, and seemingly unconnected events," and Fénelon declared that "the main point is to place the reader at the heart of things and to reveal to him the links among them."[20]

The aesthetic character of the proposed reform of historiography is made particularly clear in the preface written by Jean-Jacques Garnier (1729–1805), Inspector of the Collège de France, for his revised edition and continuation (1770–78) of the popular *Histoire de France* of the ex-Jesuit abbé Paul-François Velly (1709–59). Velly's history,

18. *Oeuvres* (Versailles and Paris: J. A. Lebel, A. Leclère, 1820–30), 21:230.
19. *Lectures,* 2:261 (Lecture 35).
20. Montesquieu, "Quelques réflexions sur les Lettres persanes," (1754), in Montesquieu, *Oeuvres complètes* (Paris: Editions du Seuil, 1964), p. 62; Blair, *Lectures,* 2:262; Fénelon, *Lettre,* in *Oeuvres,* 21:230.

which was the basis of successive revised editions in the course of the eighteenth century, was itself essentially a revision of a traditional royalist history-of-France, the function of which was basically the legitimation of political authority, and the fundamental form of which goes back to the medieval *Grandes Chroniques*. "The history of France, from the fifteenth to the nineteenth century," Philippe Ariès remarks, "is not a series of episodes whose mutual relations and relative importance are subject to the scrutiny and revision of the scholar, the critic, the philosopher. . . . There is a history of France as there are subjects of tragedies and of operas, as there is an Orpheus or a Phèdre which each artist exploits in his own way. It is a subject: not History, but the History-of-France, which each generation rewrites in its own style and according to its own manner."[21] Garnier's proposal, which he himself did not carry out effectively, involved above all reshaping that history aesthetically, giving it the form of a literary narrative rather than of a folktale. He did propose, like Sorel, Mézeray, and others before him, that patently "legendary" material (i.e., material unacceptable to a public for which "vraisemblance" had become a condition of acceptance) be scrapped, and that material on laws, customs, and the arts be introduced, but this implied no more fundamental a change in the historical account than the addition, today, of some mention of demography or nutrition in works whose form remains obstinately the one prescribed by traditional political history.

The essence of Garnier's proposals was aesthetic. There is a clear echo of Aristotle in the statement that "a fact is any kind of event whatsoever; one may be completely ignorant of its causes and relations. . . . An action, on the other hand, has necessarily a beginning, a middle, and an end." Garnier criticized the earliest historians of France for having simply gathered isolated facts and arranged them in chronological order, without any concern for possible internal relations among them. Those who came after them, he went on, simply followed the path that had been traced out for them and were satisfied if they could enrich the existing story with some new anecdote, or correct a date. "Every one has tried to add to the discoveries already made, to substitute a pure and sometimes decorative style for the gross and semibarbarous language of our old chroniclers, but nobody has thought of altering a fundamentally vicious plan." Garnier's own suggestion involved the same kind of reordering that Voltaire and

21. Philippe Ariès, *Le Temps de l'histoire* (Monaco: Editions du Rocher, 1954), p. 194.

Fénelon had demanded. The historian "should find a luminous point of view from which the reader could easily allow his gaze to embrace the entire sequence of facts, a pregnant principle of which each particular fact would be only a development or consequence." Isolated facts that cannot be related to the principal action should be treated in digressions if they are important in themselves, and simply abandoned if they are not. In this way, "a reader can traverse a long succession of centuries without weariness or boredom; he sees the facts follow one another in their natural order; in a way he knows them in advance, since with the help of the principles with which he has been provided and which are constantly in his mind, he can already divine what will be the outcome of such and such a combination of events. He puts himself in the place of the principal actors, and experiences, in part, the passions that agitated them."[22]

The recurrent comparison of historical narrative with *peinture d'histoire* and the allusions to the requirements of perspective that are so characteristic of eighteenth-century discussions of history, whether by obscure figures like Garnier, or by eminent ones, such as Voltaire and Marmontel (see especially the latter's article "Histoire," in his *Eléments de littérature*), point clearly to the nature of the goal neoclassical historiography set itself: to recast the mere succession or juxtaposition of chronicle narrative in the same way that the masters of perspective had transformed painting. Instead of being placed in immediate relation to the object of narration, the reader, like the narrator, was to be placed at a distance from it, so that it appeared to him as if it were situated in a framed and closed space upon which he could look out, as through a window. As it was unfolded, the narrative would assume the characteristics of a painting or tableau which could be embraced in a simultaneous vision similar to that enjoyed by the eye as it moves over the canvas. While following the sequence of events, in other words, the reader was to anticipate the entire plot, so that each event as it was narrated would fit into its allotted place. Thus the *fortschreitende Handlung* of epic narrative, in Lessing's terms (*Laokoon,* XV), would be gathered up constantly in the *stehende Handlung* of the visual arts. At the same time, by occupying the proper point from which the narrative was intended to be "viewed," the reader, like the art lover looking at a *peinture d'histoire,* would perceive correctly the groupings of the figures and the relation of the details to the principal figures or action. The viewer standing close up

22. J. J. Garnier, ed., *Histoire de France, par M. l'abbé Velly* (Paris: Saillant, 1770), 1: xxii–xxv (editor's Foreword).

against the canvas or the reader closely concerned with the events being narrated (the aristocratic reader, for instance, who knows the characters personally or has himself participated in the action) would see the details, and might well find pleasure in them, but the reader standing back from the canvas or the story (the bourgeois who does not make the political or military history that is the principal object of historical narratives, the philosopher, posterity, the universal reader) would alone dominate the entire work, discerning the order and hierarchy of its parts, and so be able truly to *read* the canvas before him. The ideal reader of the eighteenth century is the detached, philosophical observer, the bourgeois spectator, who masters history by reducing it to order or theory, not the actor on the stage or those too close to the action to be able to view it as a self-contained entity, complete in itself, an object removed from the continuity of reality.

In neoclassical historiography the part is thus subordinated to the whole, the particular to the general, the syntagmatic to the paradigmatic. What the reader of history observes is the unfolding of a distinct, autonomous action, which is already inscribed, from the beginning, in the elements that constitute it. "From his position at the origin of things," Fontenelle wrote of an ideal history, "the reader would entertain himself by contemplating the consequences that he had already foreseen; for once the general principles have been grasped, everything that can possibly come of them can be embraced in a universal view, and the details are only an entertaining diversion, which may even, on occasion, be dispensed with, being excessively facile and of no great utility."[23] History here is turned into destiny, and time made into the medium in which a timeless order unfolds.

Meanwhile, at the other end of the spectrum, the novel was giving itself an air of history and offering itself to the reader as reportage, the order of which is prescribed by events as they occur, not by art. In Diderot's *Jacques le fataliste* the narrator exposes the banality of the reader's expectations and takes delight in frustrating them in the name of the arbitrariness and unpredictability of a reality that supposedly accompanies its narration instead of preceding it. There is no *point de vue lumineux* here, and the grand perspective of the historian has become Jacques's *grand rouleau*. With his faith that events always follow familiar patterns, the reader in Diderot's text resembles Jacques's master, of whom it is said early in the novel: "He has eyes like you and me; but most of the time it is by no means certain that he

---

23. "Essai sur l'histoire" (ca. 1690), in *Histoire des Oracles, Du Bonheur, Essai sur l'histoire, Dialogues des Morts* (Paris: Union générale des éditions, 1966), p. 160.

looks." In other words, his ideas about the world he lives in derive from mental schemata, not from observation. To the master's belief that he can fully discern the essential and unchanging features of an order that happens to suit him very well, Jacques responds by pointing to the great scroll of destiny, which being infinite, cannot ever be totalized, and so guarantees the unpredictability of the historical order. In a similar way, the narrator opposes the richness and arbitrariness of "reality" to the orderly and ordering categories of the mind and of literary convention.

But Diderot's analysis of the relation of history and fiction, or arbitrariness and order, is not settled in favor of the former.[24] The text leaves no doubt that the writer is inventing even when he claims to be following reality, and that this claim is itself a fiction, a move in a rhetorical and artistic strategy, not a step outside the world of art and rhetoric. Writing always implies selection, organization, signification, or the making of meaning. In *Le Neveu de Rameau,* Rameau fills the slot that Jacques filled in the other work: he is receptive to experience, adaptable to circumstances as they present themselves, endlessly changeable. Moi, the philosopher, on the other hand, fills the slot of the master: he is a dreamer and a schemer, who imagines he controls his destiny but turns out to be completely cut off from the world—Diogenes masturbating in his barrel. And yet it is not Rameau but Moi who, as narrator, devises, emplots, and composes the entire dialogue in which Rameau is by far the livelier and more colorful participant.

Schiller, who knew his Diderot well, expresses in a striking formula the essential tension that runs through nearly all Diderot's reflection on science and art:

> The more multiform the cultivation of the sensibility is, the more variable it is, and the greater surface it offers to phenomena, the more world does Man *apprehend,* the more potentialities does he develop within himself; the greater the strength and depth that the personality achieves, and the more freedom the reason gains, the more world does Man *comprehend,* the more form does he create outside himself. Thus his culture will consist of two things: first providing the receptive faculty with the most multifarious contacts with the world, and as regards feeling, pushing passivity to its fullest extent; secondly, securing for the determining faculty the fullest independence from the receptive, and as

24. An essential text on this subject, in my view, is the delightful fable of the cuckoo and the nightingale recounted at Holbach's by Abbé Galiani and reported by Diderot in a letter to Sophie Volland of October 20, 1760 (*Lettres à Sophie Volland,* ed. André Babelon [Paris: Gallimard, 1938], 1:151–53).

regards reason, pushing activity to its fullest extent. Where both qualities are united, Man will combine the greatest fullness of existence with
the utmost self-dependence and freedom, and instead of abandoning
himself to the world he will rather draw it into himself with the whole
infinity of its phenomena, and subject it to the unity of his reason.[25]

Not surprisingly, Schiller's view of history includes the same po-
larities that characterized fictional narrative for Diderot. In his inaugural lecture at Jena in May 1789, "What Is Universal History and
Why Do We Study It?," Schiller distinguishes carefully between the
course of the world ("der Gang der Welt") and the course of world
history ("der Gang der Weltgeschichte"), between events and their
history. Only some of the waves on the immense river of the past are
visible to the historian, says Schiller, and, in addition, the historian's
perception is determined by his own situation, so that events are
often torn out of the dense and complex web of their contemporary
relations in order to be set in a pattern constructed retrospectively by
the historian. The order of history is not given, it is constructed by us
as a kind of wager on the rationality and intelligibility of historical

25. *Letters on the Aesthetic Education of Man,* Letter 13, quoted from the translation by Reginald Snell (London: Routledge and Kegan Paul, 1954), p. 69. The two poles
defined by Diderot and Schiller—the empirical and the rational, the chaotic fullness of
reality and the skinny order of the mind—have continued to figure prominently in
reflection on history, with preference going now to one, now to the other. In an early
essay Kierkegaard expresses the opposition in terms of history and philosophy and
expects the latter to include and master the former, though without doing violence to it:
"The observer should be an eroticist, no feature, no moment should be indifferent to
him; on the other hand, he should also feel his own preponderance, but only use it to
assist the phenomenon to its complete manifestation. Even though the observer brings
the concept with him, therefore, it is essential that the phenomenon remain inviolate
and that the concept be seen coming into existence through the phenomenon. . . .
Philosophy relates to history as a confessor to the penitent, and, . . . as the penitent
individual is able to rattle off the fateful events of his life chronologically, even recite
them entertainingly, but cannot himself see through them, so history is able to proclaim
with pathos the rich full life of the race, but must leave its explanation to the elder
[philosophy]" (*The Concept of Irony,* trans. Lee M. Capel [London: Collins, 1966], pp.
47–48). More recently, the other view was taken by Albert Guérard in an essay in
which he argues that the literary models of the historian prevent him from ever en-
countering the real: "History, as presented by historians, is a well-made play: not a
pageantry of detached episodes, but a situation, with exposition, growth, crisis. . . .
History is legend, symbol, and myth. Its rules are not those of political economy but of
epic drama. Between history and fiction . . . there is a profound identity which sets
them apart from statistical science, social or physical, and from the pure logic of
mathematics." Guérard acknowledges that there are differences, "but the boundaries
are hard to trace" ("Millennia," in *Generalization in Historical Writing,* ed. A. Riaza-
novsky and B. Riznik [Philadelphia: Univ. of Pennsylvania Press, 1963], pp. 167–206).

existence, and because—especially if we are eighteenth-century Deists—we can scarcely think of the universe except in terms of orderly design. "One after another phenomena begin to withdraw from the sphere of blind chance, or lawless liberty, and to find their places as concordant parts of a coherent whole (which to be sure, is present only as an idea in the historian's mind). . . . The historian thus draws that harmony forth from himself, and transplants it, outside himself, in the order of external things, that is to say, he brings to the course of the world a rational end, and a teleological principle to world history." He applies this harmonious order to every phenomenon presented by the great theater of the world, and finds that many confirm it and many contradict it. As long as he cannot establish all the links in the chain, the question of the order of history remains unresolved for him, but "that opinion carries the day for him, which offers the highest satisfaction to the understanding and to the heart the greatest felicity."[26]

The polarity of the receptive faculty and the determining faculty, of the world and of reason, or, as we might also say, of the syntagmatic and the paradigmatic, is thus in no way identical, in the neoclassical period, with the polarity of history and fiction. It operates *within* both. Fictional writing is constantly questioning existing fictional conventions, and for centuries it did so by appealing to history. But historical writing operates in the same way: every attempt to devise an order different from that of pure chronicle involved an appeal to the order of art—of fictional narrative or of drama. And correspondingly, when the intention was to reject a highly structured model of historical narrative, emphasis was again placed on the syntagmatic, and on the historian's task as simple reporter or eyewitness. The little-known but extremely interesting work of Prosper de Barante, an outstanding member of the narrative school of historians during the French Restoration, is an illuminating case of a move in this direction. The very title of Barante's work, *Histoire des ducs de Bourgogne de la maison de Valois* (1824–26), signals the predominance of the syntagmatic: the unity of the elements of the narrative lies in genealogical relations, relations of pure succession. In contrast, Augustin Thierry's *Histoire de la conquête de l'Angleterre par les Normands,* which appeared in 1825, announces in its title the unifying role of the general concept of conquest, an important historical category at the time and one that had been the subject of an influential

26. "Was heisst und zu welchem Ende studiert man Universalgeschichte?," in *Schillers Werke* (Nationalausgabe, Weimar, 1970), 17:372–74.

essay by Benjamin Constant. In his Introduction, Thierry explicitly drew attention to the paradigmatic aspect of his narrative. His history of the Norman Conquest, he said, was a model of all the histories of the European countries. Yet Thierry was in no way critical of narrative history. On the contrary, he is rightly considered one of the leaders of the narrative school. But he emphasized the paradigmatic aspect of the historical text as well as the syntagmatic one.

Although at times historical narrative and fictional narrative may seem to have been straining in opposite directions, they have both traditionally accepted the essential conditions of classical narrative and have operated within the framework these provide. The framing of narrative, the establishment of a special time of narrative discontinuous with the time of the narrator's own telling is signaled, according to Emile Benveniste, by the use of a certain set of verb tenses, notably the simple past or aorist, assisted by the imperfect and the pluperfect. These tenses constitute in this respect a system, and the present, the future, the perfect—all the tenses with the exception of the simple past—constitute another. The tenses of the second system all maintain a relation to the present and direct attention to the subject, to the act of speaking (*l'énonciation*), and to the present relation between narrator or speaker and reader or listener, rather than exclusively to the events being narrated (*l'énoncé*).[27] The use of the appropriate tense system is a condition of narrative, whether the latter is presented as true or as fictional, whether it is, in Voltaire's words "le récit des faits donnés pour vrais" or "le récit des faits donnés pour faux."[28] Despite his efforts to subvert the traditional form of narrative, in *Jacques le fataliste,* by foregrounding the narrator and the act of telling, and by presenting the act of telling as contemporary with what is being told, Diderot did not succeed in eliminating the past tense itself even from the narrative of his frame story. He could illuminate the processes of telling and reading or listening, but he

27. Emile Benveniste, "La Relation de temps dans le verbe français" (1959), in *Problèmes de linguistique générale* (Paris: Gallimard, 1966), pp. 237–50. "[Facts] are characterized as past," Benveniste writes, "by the mere fact of being registered and enunciated in temporal expressions of past time." And, "We shall define historical narrative as that mode of enunciation which excludes every 'autobiographical' linguistic form. The historian will never say *I* or *you, here* or *now,* because he will never make use of the formal devices of discourse, which consist, in the first place, in the relation of the first and second persons—*I:you.*"

28. "Histoire," *Encyclopédie,* Vol. 8 (1765), in *Oeuvres,* 19:346. Cf. Benveniste, "La Relation," p. 240, n. 1: "The historical enunciation of events is, of course, independent of their 'objective' truth. All that counts is the 'historical' intention of the writer."

could not actually fuse the two planes of enunciation, which Benveniste characterizes as *histoire* and *discours*. These, with their respective verbal systems, remain clearly distinguishable throughout his text. *Jacques,* moreover, includes many traditionally told tales within the frame story, as though to emphasize that the construction of intelligible models of experience is both necessary and inevitable, and that the revelation of the role of the narrator in their production and of the reader in their interpretation can make us aware of what we are doing but cannot alter the actual form in which we do it.

By means of the "discourse" with which he is free to accompany his narrative of events, however, the historian and the novelist alike can comment on the action being related and orient the reader's attitude toward it. Not surprisingly, at any given time there tend to be many points of resemblance between the discourse of historians and that of novelists.

The characteristic feature of eighteenth-century fiction is the ironic distance most eighteenth-century novels establish between the narrator and the narrative, and the complicity they set up between the reader and the narrator over against the narrative—that is to say, the clear distinction they make between *discours* and *histoire,* and the privilege they accord to the former. This is also what characterizes Voltaire, Hume, and Gibbon as historians. The Enlightenment historian tells his tale in the same conditions as the eighteenth-century novelist, and, like him, engages the reader with him as ironic spectator of the historical scene or tableau. The ultimate unifying center of eighteenth-century historical writing, it has been said, is the narrator himself rather than the narrative of events:[29] the latter exists largely as a pretext for "philosophical" commentary, and for the sake of the community of "philosophers" that this commentary was expected to establish between narrator and reader, and among readers. History, in this important respect, was not essentially different from fiction, and d'Alembert's remark that the writings of Tacitus "would not lose much if we were to consider them only as the first and truest of philosophical novels"[30] probably did not seem as odd or shocking

---

29. See Leo Braudy, *Narrative Form in History and Fiction: Hume, Fielding, and Gibbon* (Princeton: Princeton Univ. Press, 1970). The historians of the Restoration were already aware of this characteristic of their predecessors' work. According to Barante ("De l'histoire," p. 48), the unity of the eighteenth-century historical narrative "results from the concerns of the author. . . . The past is decomposed, torn to pieces, rendered lifeless: only the author's idea remains alive and animated, and it is that idea that pulls us along."

30. "Réflexions sur l'histoire," *Oeuvres* (Paris: Bastien, an XIII [1805]), 4:195.

to the eighteenth-century reader as it does to us, or at least as it must have done to the serious nineteenth-century reader. Voltaire also distinguished between the value of an intelligible model—which fiction can presumably be as well as history—and merely factually true accounts. "We have to make distinctions among the errors of historians. A false date, a wrong name, are only material for a volume of *errata*. If the main body of the work is otherwise true, if the interests, the motives, the events have been faithfully unfolded, we have a well-made statue which can be faulted for some slight imperfection of a fold in the drapery."[31]

Voltaire himself never justified his constant correction and revision of his historical writings, and his tireless seeking out of new information, except on the grounds that a healthy respect for truth was generally a good mental hygiene. The overall pattern, in Voltaire's histories, was always being subverted by individual acts, the ideal universal truth by particular events, the general maxim by the exceptions to it, and the endless confrontation of the particular and the general led, in Voltaire's case, not to a solution at the level of the object, but to one at the level of the subject—to irony. It reinforced and justified the central position of the narrator, and privileged the act of thinking "as a Philosopher" about history and about the problematics of history over the matter of the objective truth or otherwise of the narrative. What was important was not the truth of the narrative so much as the activity of reflecting about the narrative, including that of reflecting about its truth. History, in the eighteenth century, raised questions and created conditions in which the individual subject, the critical reason, could exercise and assert its freedom. It did not present itself as an objectively true and therefore compelling discovery of reality itself. On the contrary, its truth and validity were always problematic, provoking the reader's reflection and thus renewing his freedom. In an important sense, therefore, historical narrative and fictional narrative were constructed in fundamentally similar ways in the eighteenth century.

It would not be too difficult, in all probability, to show that nineteenth-century historical narrative also shares important structural features with nineteenth-century fictional narrative, notably the explicit rejection of the clear Enlightenment separation of object and subject, past and present, narrative and commentary or discourse, and the attempt to make them continuous with each other. The domi-

31. *Siècle de Louis XIV*, Supplement, Part 1 (Paris: Garnier-Flammarion, 1966), 2:320.

nant feature of both fictional and historical narrative in the nineteenth century is the replacement of the overt eighteenth-century persona of the narrator by a covert narrator, and the corresponding presentation of the narrative as unproblematic, absolutely binding. The nineteenth-century narrator appears as a privileged reporter reconstructing what happened. The historical text is thus not presented as a model to be discussed, criticized, accepted, or repudiated by the free and inquiring intellect, but as the inmost form of the real, binding, and inescapable. In the struggle to establish *philosophie,* in other words, the eighteenth-century historian accepted his ideological function proudly; in the nineteenth century, the historian's ideological function and the rhetoric he deployed in its service were denied, in the deepest sense, since the historian himself did not recognize them.

In our own time, there appear to be correspondences between developments in historiography and certain developments in modern fiction—among them the repudiation of realism, the collapse of the subject or character as an integrated and integrating entity, and an increasingly acute awareness of the fundamental logic or syntax of narrative and of the constraints and opportunities it provides. In a wise and entertaining book published after his death, Sigfried Kracauer took malicious pleasure in showing how even an eminent historian like Henri Pirenne used time-worn rhetorical tricks to bring together relatively discontinuous persons and events in a single, continuous, and unified narrative.[32] The relations between different historical series

32. *History: The Last Things before the Last* (New York: Oxford Univ. Press, 1969). The relevant chapter in this volume first appeared as "General History and the Aesthetic Approach," in *Die nicht mehr schönen Künste,* ed. H. R. Jauss (Munich: Fink, 1968), pp. 109–27, notably pp. 120–21. Blair (*Lectures,* 2:273) had already noted that "much . . . will depend on the proper management of transitions, which forms one of the chief ornaments of this kind of writing." Cf. H. Stuart Hughes, in *History as Art and as Science* (New York: Harper & Row, 1964), pp. 70–71: "Historians have developed a myriad of literary devices for gliding over what they do not adequately know or understand. With more schematic history, the gaps yawn embarrassingly wide: in narrative prose they can be artfully concealed."

The power of narrative order, and at the same time its distance from "reality", is graphically conveyed by the narrator of Claude Simon's novel *Le Vent* (Paris: Editions de Minuit, 1957), in a passage (pp. 9–10) whose anxious tone and pessimistic emphasis are in striking contrast to the calm optimism of Schiller's essay on universal history of a century and a half before. The narrator is describing his difficulty in interpreting a story that is being told to him: "And as the notary was talking to me, was starting out again—for maybe the tenth time—on that story (or at least what he knew of it, or at least imagined about it, for of the events that had been going on for seven months he had, like every one else, like the heroes, the actors in the events themselves, only the fragmentary, incomplete knowledge that can be pieced together from a number of rapid (political actions, institutions, economics, nutrition, climate, population, regions, towns, language, literature, philosophy, etc.) now appear problematic at least, since time is no longer assumed to be a uniform medium in which historical events occur or historical phenomena have their existence, and which in itself establishes a continuity among these diverse phenomena, but seems rather to be multiform, constituted differently by the phenomena placed in series. The same is true of space.[33] Braudel's three-level distinction of *histoire événementielle, histoire conjoncturale,* and *histoire de longue durée* is now familiar to a wide public. Earlier, Lucien Febvre had called for a historiography which, instead of being located in a supposedly even and objective time-flow (and thereby in fact positing such a time-flow), would select moments of crisis, collision, and breakdown. Discontinuity, in short, rather than continuity, was to be placed at the heart of history as it had been placed already at the heart of fiction.[34]

---

images, themselves imperfectly apprehended by the eyes, of words poorly understood, of sensations ill-defined, and the whole thing vague, full of holes, of gaps which imagination and a logic of approximation did their best to make up for with a series of risky deductions—risky, but not necessarily false, for either everything is only chance, and in that case the thousand and one versions, the thousand and one faces of a story are also, or rather just are, constitute the story, since such it is, was, and remains in the consciousness of those who lived it, suffered it, endured it, were diverted by it, or else reality itself is invested with a life of its own, high and mighty, independent of our perceptions and therefore of our knowledge and, above all, of our appetite for logical connections—and in that case the effort to find it, to discover it, to dislodge it, may be as futile, as disappointing as those children's toys, those nests of dolls from Central Europe, each one set inside another, each one containing, disclosing a smaller one, until you arrive at something tiny, minuscule, insignificant: nothing at all; and now, now that it's all over, the effort to report, to reconstruct what happened is a little like trying to glue the scattered, incomplete bits and pieces of a broken mirror back together again, making clumsy efforts to fit them together, and coming up with an incoherent, derisive, idiotic result, in which only our mind perhaps, or rather our pride, enjoins us, on pain of madness and against all evidence, to find at all costs a logical sequence of causes and effects where all that reason can discern is a straying, ourselves being heaved about from all sides, like a cork adrift on the water, aimless, sightless, endeavoring only to stay afloat, and suffering, and dying in the end, and then that it's over. . . .) as the notary was talking, then, I couldn't help trying to imagine that other, the person who had provided the material for the town's storytellers."

33. See Lucien Febvre, *La Terre et l'évolution humaine* (Paris: Renaissance du livre, 1922).

34. See also Kracauer, "General History," p. 122: "All these devices and techniques [for establishing transitions] follow a harmonizing tendency—which is to say that their underlying intentions flagrantly conflict with those of contemporary art. Joyce, Proust, and Virginia Woolf, the pioneers of the modern novel, no longer care to render biographical developments and chronological sequences after the manner of the older novel; on the contrary, they resolutely decompose (fictitious) continuity over time. . . .

Above all, the attack on historical realism, begun in the early nineteenth century, has become more intense and more radical. Nineteenth-century philosophers challenged the naïve realism of the classical historians and emphasized the place of subjectivity in historical knowledge. For many who reflected on the problems of historical knowledge, the fact that the knower is himself involved in the historical process as a maker of history and is thus unable to achieve the "objective" view aspired to by the natural scientist was the very condition of historical knowledge, as opposed to knowledge of the natural world. There was no question, however, that the historian's aim was to know and to reveal the reality of the past. Only this reality was now thought of as at once given and concealed, so that the historian's job was, as Humboldt had said at the beginning of the century in his essay *Die Aufgabe des Geschichtschreibers,* to divine (*ahnden*) it. The historian reached through to past reality by a process of divination or symbolic interpretation of the evidence. Recent reflection on history, like recent reflection on literature, however, has tended increasingly to question the mimetic ideal itself.

In an article first published in 1943, Lucien Febvre recalled that in 1860, in the flush of the first successes of organic chemistry, Berthelot was already proclaiming that "chemistry makes its object." According to Febvre, Berthelot claimed that unlike the natural and historical sciences, whose object is given in advance, independently of the scientist's will and action, chemistry, like art, has the power to create a multitude of artificial substances similar to natural ones. It is thereby released from bondage to the object. In Febvre's view, however,

> this distinction between chemistry and the other sciences is no longer valid. All scientists now define Science as creation, present it as "creating its object," and insist on the constant play of the scientist's will and activity. Such is the climate of Science today. A climate that has nothing in common with the Science of yesterday—the Science of the days

---

Modern art radically challenges the artistic ideals from which the general historian draws his inspiration—from which he must draw it to establish his genre. . . . " In an earlier text, "Biography as a Neobourgeois Art Form," originally published in 1930, Kracauer had already argued that the popularity of history, and especially of historical biography in the interwar years, needed to be interpreted in the context of the collapse, after World War I, of the bourgeois idea of world order and of the autonomous, coherent self. In this context "history emerges as a solid land mass out of the ocean of the formless and the unformable." The meaning of biography in particular is "that in the chaos of contemporary artistic experiments, it represents the only apparently necessary prose form" ("Die Biographie als neubürgerliche Kunstform," in *Das Ornament der Masse* [Frankfurt a/M.: Suhrkamp, 1963], pp. 75–80).

when I was twenty. That Science and the postulates on which it was founded have been thoroughly shaken, criticized, left behind. Scientists gave them up years ago and replaced them with others. So I ask a question—one simple question: Are we historians alone going to continue to recognize them as valid? . . . Is it not time to stop, once and for all, looking to the "sciences" of fifty years ago to shore up and justify our theories—since the sciences of fifty years ago are–no more than memories and ghosts.[35]

In a similar vein, it has often been argued by philosophers that the historian's objects are not unproblematically situated on the other side of the evidence, as it were, but constructs, whose function is to account for the present evidence. "George Washington," one such argument runs, "enjoys at present the epistemological status of an electron: each is an entity postulated for the purpose of giving coherence to our present experience, and each is unobservable by us." According to the same argument, "the forthright empiricism which has generally prevailed in the historical trade" has laudable objectives,

but its view of the process by which historical knowledge is attained is naive. In holding that external and internal criticism yield statements from which facts are determined, and that the function of interpretation is to account for all, or a preselected few, of these facts, it badly distorts the actual practice of historians. In fact, interpretation enters at every step along the way. External criticism is really a process of testing classificatory hypotheses about objects and so depends upon such interpretative hypotheses being made. Similarly, the attribution of meaning and reference to an inscription is an interpretative or hypothetical process. Historical facts are not established from pure data—they are postulated to explain characteristics of the data. Thus the sharp division between fact and interpretation upon which the classical view insisted and which the revisionists have accepted, does not exist.[36]

35. *Combats pour l'histoire* (Paris: Armand Colin, 1953), pp. 30–31.
36. Murray G. Murphey, *Our Knowledge of the Historical Past* (Indianapolis: Bobbs-Merrill, 1973), pp. 16, 63–64. A similar argument, more closely related to historical practice at the present time, is developed by Michel de Certeau in an article roughly contemporary with Murphey's book. "The transformation of 'archivistics' has been the departure point and the condition of a new kind of history. . . . I shall take only one example: the advent of the computer. François Furet has shown some of the effects produced by 'the constitution of new archives stored on punchcards': signification is a function of a series here, and not of a relation to a given 'reality'; only those problems that have been formally set up prior to being programmed can be objects of historical research, and so on. Yet this is but one particular element, a symptom in a way, of a vaster scientific institution. Contemporary analysis has overwhelmed the procedures associated with the type of 'symbolic analysis' which has prevailed since Romanticism and which sought to *recognize* a sense that was at once *given* and *concealed:* . . . . The

The historian appears here as someone who attempts coolly to resolve problems that are absolutely external to him. But many writers have emphasized the important role played by the historian's imagination, his concerns as an individual and as a social being, and even by his unconscious, both in the determination of the problem to be studied, and in the shaping of the historical narrative. Hayden White quotes H. I. Marrou, the historian, who, as "Henry Davenson," author of a valuable *Introduction à la chanson française* (1941), knows a great deal about poetry: "If the historian is a man and if he actually reaches the level of history (if he is not a mere academician, busy selecting materials for an eventual history), he will not pass his time in splitting hairs over questions which do not keep anyone from sleeping. . . . He will pursue, in his dialogue with the past, the elaboration of *the* question which *does* keep *him* from sleeping, the central problem of his existence, the solution of which involves his life and entire person."[37] Without going so far as to claim with Unamuno that "the tyrants depicted by Tacitus were all himself,"[38] Alain Besancon argues that all historical research is in some measure "recherche de soi-même . . . introspection." According to Besançon, "the fundamental operation of the sciences of human behavior is not the observation of the subject by the observer. It is the analysis of their interaction in a situation in which both are at one and the same time subjects and observers." It follows that Besançon is skeptical of certain orientations of contemporary historiography, which he identifies as alibis for the genuinely fruitful but disturbing encounter of the historian with the texts of the past. "The piling up of factual refer-

practice of modern historical analysis consists of constructing 'models,' 'substituting for the study of concrete phenomena the study of objects constituted by their definition,' judging the scientific value of those objects by the 'field of questions' to which they permit us to look for answers and by the answers they provide, and, finally, 'determining the limits within which a given model can provide meanings' " ("L'Opération historique," in *Faire de l'histoire: nouveaux problèmes,* ed. Jacques le Goff and Pierre Nora [Paris: Gallimard, 1974], p. 23). De Certeau's essay brings out the radical character of contemporary historical "science" with respect to the earlier German idealist critique of naïve realism. The German idealists still aimed at the perception of a (God-) given reality; they wished to recognize and accommodate the role of subjectivity in the process of perception, but they did not question that "reality" was what was to be perceived.

37. "From the Logic of History to an Ethic for the Historian," *Cross-Currents* (1961), quoted by Hayden White in "The Politics of Contemporary Philosophy of History," *Clio,* 3 (1973), 35–54.

38. Miguel de Unamuno, "Comment on écrit un roman" (French trans. by Jean Cassou), *Mercure de France,* 15 (1926), 15.

ences in card-index boxes, the complete count of the number of pairs of shoes exported from Livradois to Forez, utilizing higher mathematics and computers, become so many maneuvers whose aim is less the advancement of scientific knowledge than the removal of the specific anguish that attaches to the act of creation." In the end, what historical study produces, Besançon insists, is not unified or total knowledge of the past or of some fragment of it, but a *book,* a text. The unity of history lies in the books written by the great historians. "If we ponder over Fustel's *La Cité antique,* Bloch's *Société féodale,* whereas we only consult corresponding works, it is because between one group of writings and another, there is the same kind of difference as between the works of Dostoyevsky and those of Eugène Sue, which inspired them."[39]

One of the most effective and radical criticisms of historical realism has been made by highlighting the linguistic existence of historical narratives, by emphasizing that history constructs its objects, and that its objects are objects of language, rather than entities of which words are in some way copies. From this point of view, the *battle of Gettysburg,* for instance, does not designate unproblematically something solid in reality that is prior to any naming of it. The semiology of history, moreover, is more complex than that of language itself. In historical writing, the signs of language become signifiers in a secondary system elaborated by the historian. What already has meaning at the level of language becomes an empty form again until, being brought into relation with an historically definable *signifié,* or concept, it constitutes a new sign at a different level of meaning. Historical discourse thus has the character of a language constructed out of material that is itself already language. Roland Barthes has been especially critical of every failure to acknowledge the linguistic character of the historical text, and of a persistent tendency to see the text as the mere copy of another existence situated in an extrastructural field, namely "the real." "Like every discourse that claims to be 'realist,' " Barthes writes, "historical discourse believes it knows a semantic system constituted by only two terms—the signifier and the referent."[40] It thus dispenses with a term that is essential to language

---

39. "Vers une histoire psychanalytique" (orig. pub. in *Annales,* 1969), in *Histoire et expérience du moi* (Paris: Flammarion, 1971), pp. 66, 68, 70, 85. Besançon's position bears a certain resemblance to that of some late-nineteenth-century German philosophers, such as Rickert, the unconscious being substituted, in Besançon's case, for the philosophers' spirit or *Geist.*

40. "Le Discours de l'histoire," *Information sur les sciences sociales,* 6, No. 4 (1967), 74.

and fundamental to every imaginary structure—the *signifié*. Far from the world of things founding and supporting the world of signs, as classical historical discourse appears to suppose—Barthes objects—it seems rather that the world of signs constitutes and calls into existence the world of things. Reality, in sum, is human; it is always that which we make signify, never a mere given.

Those historians who have been most willing to recognize the role of imagination in the writing of history or the proximity of history and fiction, have also, understandably, been most concerned to distinguish between the two, and to establish the specificity of history. Though there appears to be a certain longing to found the difference in the historical narrative's continued dependency on the real world, the specificity of history can probably be more easily defined in terms of its own rules, its own system, than in terms of a direct relation of dependency upon the real world. R. G. Collingwood, for instance, proposes three rules or conditions for history—that the historian, unlike the novelist, must localize his story in time and place; that all history must be consistent with itself, since there is only one historical world, whereas fictional universes, being autonomous, need not agree, and cannot clash; and that the historical imagination is not completely free but is bound to work from "evidence."[41]

Of these rules, the first seems to be an aspect of the second. Space and time are not absolute but are themselves defined by the historian, so that the first rule really reads: the historian's space and time must be consistent with the space and time of other historians. Interestingly, many novelists, anxious to give an air of history to their fictions, accept the space and time of the historian and try to observe this rule wherever their narratives do impinge on those of the historian. Space and time, in other words, do not appear to be objective realities that found the historian's work and differentiate it from the imaginary writings of the novelists, but rather a particular space and time act as signals to the reader that a work is to be regarded as history. The specificity of the text, in short, is not established by something outside it but by its own system. The second rule—the historian must verify whether his story tallies with the stories of other historians and with the documentary record—rests on the premise that the historical world is one, and this may be seen as a regulative idea rather than a statement of fact. The consistency rule suggests that the goal and purpose of history may well be, at certain times

41. *The Idea of History* (Oxford: Clarendon, 1946; rpt. New York: Oxford Univ. Press, 1956), p. 246.

anyway, to establish or affirm the unity and coherency of the historical world or of the part of it being related, but the rule itself does not seem to have any objective justification. Once again, the specificity of the text is not established by something outside it, but by its own system. The fact that a story is presented as consonant with other stories and verifiable in relation to them establishes it as history.[42] The rule founds the historical world; it is not derived from it. Moreover, it is still possible for the historian, without infringing the consistency rule, to emplot the "same" events in different stories, and to construct different events from the same evidence. The consistency rule, it seems, limits what the historian may do, rather as conventional ideas of probability limit what the novelist may do; but within these limits, the historian may propose a variety of configurations and the rules according to which these are engendered may well be the same as the rules by which fictional narratives are engendered. The simplest of events, after all, is itself a story, the interpretation of which involves a larger story of which it is part, so that history could be envisaged as a complex pattern of stories each of which contains another complex pattern of stories, and so on without end. There seems to be no outside of stories, no point at which they stop being stories and abut on hard particles of "facts."

Collingwood's third rule, the rule of evidence, also limits the historian rather than determines him. Collingwood himself acknowledges that it is not easy to separate evidence from the explanation and interpretation that it supports: we can only recognize evidence as evidence, he explains, because we already have a system or hypothesis in terms of which it acquires significance.[43] Once more, therefore,

42. See Michel Butor: "All writings that claim to be true have a common feature: they are always in principle verifiable. I must be able to cross-check what one source has told me with information obtained from another source, and so on indefinitely; otherwise I am in the presence of an error or a fiction. . . . Whereas the story that claims to be true is always supported by, or can appeal to some external evidence, the novel must be able to call into being on its own the subject matter of its discourse with us" ("Le Roman comme recherche," in *Essais sur le roman* [Paris: Gallimard, 1969; 1st ed. 1960], pp. 8–9).

43. "The whole perceptible world . . . is potentially and in principle evidence to the historian. It becomes actual evidence in so far as he can use it. And he cannot use it unless he comes to it with the right kind of historical knowledge. The more historical knowledge we have, the more we can learn from any given piece of evidence; if we had none, we could learn nothing. Evidence is evidence only when some one contemplates it historically. Otherwise it is merely perceived fact, historically dumb. It follows that historical knowledge can only grow out of historical knowledge; in other words, that historical thinking is an original and fundamental activity of the human mind, or, as Descartes might have said, that the idea of the past is an 'innate' idea" (*Idea of History*, p. 247).

the historian's constructive and imaginative activity is involved in the very foundations of his work. Evidence—texts, documents, artifacts—is by definition a sign, and it signifies within a system of signs. The historian's narrative is constructed not upon reality itself or upon transparent images of it, but on signifiers which the historian's own action transforms into signs. It is not historical reality itself but the present signs of the historian that limit and order the historical narrative (just as, conversely, the historical narrative limits and orders them). Almost all historians acknowledge this implicitly in the act of placing their notes—sources, evidence—at the foot of the page. The division of the historiographical page is a testimony to the discontinuity between past "reality" and the historical narrative; and those historians who have wished to create the greatest impression of continuity between their text and reality have in fact taken care to eliminate the telltale scar separating the two parts of the page.

If it was Collingwood's intention to establish the difference between fiction and history less on history's *claim* to be "true," its constant signifying that the events it relates really happened, than on some kind of effective determination of history by past reality, then it is not clear, in my view, that he has succeeded.[44]

Nevertheless, despite decades of demonstrations by philosophers and by historians themselves that history is a construct, the belief that it is an immediate representation of reality, and the historian's own complicity with this belief, have remained remarkably vigorous. Indeed, the tenacity of the belief itself is something that requires explanation. Barthes' analysis of this phenomenon is extremely pertinent to the question of the present relation of history and literature. Barthes argues that the realism of historical discourse is part of a general cultural pattern manifested in the persistent popular predilec-

---

44. In a recent study of autobiography, Philippe Lejeune bases his discrimination of fiction and autobiography on the "pact" contracted between author and reader at the outset of the work. Textual analysis alone, he claims, yields no means of distinguishing the two. "The novelist can imitate and has imitated all the devices which the autobiographer uses to convince us of the authenticity of his narrative." But if we include as part of the "text" the title page and the name of the author, a clear signal is given, which establishes the specificity of autobiography. Lejeune insists, however, that the question of *fact*—whether or not or to what extent the narrative is a true account of the life it purports to recount—must not be confused with the question of *right*—i.e., the type of contract entered into by author and reader (*Le Pacte autobiographique* [Paris: Editions du Seuil, 1975], p. 26). It seems likely that a similar "pact" binds the author and the reader of historical works: the reader is advised that the narrative is to be regarded as true and is invited to verify it by comparing it with other narratives or with other evidence.

tion for genres such as the realist novel or the diary, in the vogue of
exhibitions of antique objects of daily use, and, above all, in the
enormous development of photography, the pertinent characteristic of
which (in relation to drawing, for instance,) is precisely that it
signifies that the event or object represented *really* happened or existed.[45] For Barthes, this cultural pattern points to an alienating fe-
tishism of the "real," by which men seek to escape from their freedom and their role as makers of meaning. The "real" appears to him
as an *idol*.

The ideological burden of history is aggravated by its closeness to
what Barthes calls contemporary myth.[46] Myth, in Barthes' sense, is
a secondary system of signs which uses elements already invested
with meaning within a prior semiological system (ordinary language):
these elements become signifiers or forms in relation to the *signifiés,*
or ideological concepts, with which the mythical discourse connects
them. This is the source of the ambiguous, dissembling character of
myth. If the reader were to read myth innocently—that is, if he were
to take the elements that compose it for what they are and fail to
recognize the concept to which they point—nothing would have been
gained by proffering it to him; if, on the other hand, reading it
thoughtfully, he were to see clearly that the elements are intended to
signify the concept, it would be no more than a straightforward political proposition. What constitutes myth as myth, according to
Barthes, is precisely its avoidance of this alternative: the relation
between signifier and concept is presented as unmotivated, in some
way natural. Although it summons the reader to read it in terms of the
concepts to which the signifiers have been linked, mythical discourse
never admits that it does, or that the signifiers are arbitrarily and not
naturally linked to the *signifiés*. When challenged, it can always plead

45. See J. Snyder and N. W. Allen, "Photography, Vision, and Representation,"
Critical Inquiry, 2 (1975), 143–69. "What is truly significant about a photograph of a
horse is not really that the horse himself printed his image, or that the photograph
shows us the horse as we ourselves would (or wouldn't) have seen him, or that it
establishes something in the way of scientific truth about this horse. What is significant
(it seems to be alleged) is that *this* horse wasn't invented by some artist: this is a
picture of a *real* horse" (p. 163). Similarly, Hilton Kramer in a *New York Times* article,
"Celebrating Formalism in Photography" (December 12, 1976), states that it is "the
omnivorous appetite for the 'real' that is the primary basis for the increased popularity
that photography has lately won for itself with the art public." The relation between
historiography and photography or film is discussed in the opening pages of Kracauer,
History.

46. "Le Mythe, aujourd'hui," in *Mythologies* (Paris: Editions du Seuil, 1957), pp.
213–68.

innocence, and take refuge behind the original meaning of the signifiers in the primary system. It is thus neither brazen nor innocent: it
is, one is tempted to say, discourse *in bad faith,* founded on a shifty
refusal to clarify the relation between the signifier and the *signifié,* or
concept. "Myth," in Barthes' own words, "is read as a factual system, whereas it is a semiological system."

History appears to share a number of the features that Barthes
considers characteristic of myth, in this modern sense. It has already
been suggested that historical narrative constitutes a secondary semiological system whose elements—events, actions, etc.—already have
a meaning within the system of ordinary language, prior to being
appropriated by the secondary system and adapted to its ends. While
the language of classical historical narrative, as Barthes himself
pointed out, presents itself as a two-term system in which the *signifié*
is dispensed with and the signifier is directly linked to the referent, in
the larger context of the historical work itself—that is, of the secondary semiotic system constructed upon the primary one of language—
the supposedly direct verbal representations of events in the primary
system become signifiers in relation to the *signifiés* of the secondary
system. What is taken to be reality itself, or at least its immediate
verbal representation—rather than a sign—thus acts as the signifier in
the secondary system. As in myth, therefore, the signifier seems naturally to lead to the *signifié,* as if the latter emerged out of it and was
continuous with it, in the way that photographs, being taken as direct
visual representations of the real, appear to found their *signifié* naturally, without the intervention of any act of signifying.

Barthes is concerned to unmask the fundamental inauthenticity of
myth, which he sees proliferating over the entire domain of culture,
appropriating and turning to ideological ends every authentic expression of human creativity. Insofar as history does not point to its signifying activity, it would seem to be subject to the same criticisms that
Barthes makes of myth. From our point of view, it is interesting, therefore, that Barthes finds the strongest center of resistance to myth in
poetic language. Whereas myth fills our universe with meanings that
masquerade as natural, produced by no one, poetic language seeks to
escape from the inauthenticity of culture toward an authentic language
that will somehow recover direct contact with things, from the pseudo-
nature of a mystified and mystifying culture to a true nature.

> Whereas myth aims at ultra-signification, at the amplification of a pri-
> mary system, poetry tries to recover an infra-signification, a pre-semi-
> ological state of language; . . . its ideal . . . would be to reach not so
> much the sense of words as the sense of things themselves. That is why

it disturbs language, exaggerating to the maximum the abstract character of the concept and the arbitrariness of the sign and pushing to the
limit of the possible the relation of signifier and signified. . . . It is the
full potential of the signified that the poetic sign tries to release and
make present, in the hope of finally reaching a sort of transcendent
quality of the thing, its natural (and not its human) meaning. Whence
the essentialist aspirations of poetry, and the conviction that it alone
can grasp the thing itself—to the degree, precisely, that it aims to be an
anti-language. . . . That is why modern poetry is always affirmed as an
assassination of language, a kind of spatial, sensible analogue of silence. Poetry is the reverse of myth: myth is a semiological system that
claims to transcend itself in a factual system; poetry is a semiological
system that claims to withdraw behind itself in an essential system.[47]

Even in the case of prose, as Barthes points out, modern literature
seeks constantly to avoid being taken up in the myth of Literature.
Every literary movement of modern times has been an attempt to
reduce literary language to a simple semiological system (ordinary
language), and to repudiate Literature as a mythical sign, the sign of
Culture.

Barthes' essay on myth seems to me to shed a disquieting light on a
great deal of the historical writing of the last century and a half. After
the French Revolution, the dominant ambition of historians was to
make history—rather than fiction—the successor of epic as the repository of society's values and of its understanding of the world.
"Our age," Barante declared, "seeks in the past the reasons for
confidence in the future, and intends that the historian shall assume
the high mission of the prophet."[48] History, consequently, had to be
cleared of the stigma attaching to the "merely" successive event, the
isolated, individual episode. Historical discourse had to order individual events into episodes, individual episodes into stories, and individual stories into the single unifying and signifying history of humanity,
of civilization, and of the modern bourgeois nation-states. Barante,
who was himself most attracted by the singular, picturesque episode,
the historical *fait divers*, as it were, explained that "the writer must
show us the facts moving steadily toward a goal, he must make us
understand every step along the way. Reason is as exacting as imagination, it demands unity, and desires that its drama and its epic, the

---

47. Ibid., pp. 241–42. Barthes has maintained this position with great consistency:
see *Le Dégré zéro de l'écriture* (Paris: Editions du Seuil, 1953) and the review of
Philippe Sollers' novel *Drame* in 1965 (rpt. in *Théorie d'ensemble* [Paris: Editions du
Seuil, 1968], pp. 25–40, esp. pp. 35–36 and n. 4).
    48. Barante, "De l'histoire," p. 50.

hero of which is an idea, be also portrayed."[49] With the Romantic attempt to create the illusion that the relation between the individual event or episode reported by the historian and the concept or *signifié* with which he associates it is natural—in other words, that signification in historical writing is unmotivated, unproblematic, somehow rooted in the nature of things themselves—history comes perilously close to what Barthes describes as myth. And at the same time, in a corresponding and inverse movement, literature comes to repudiate the mythos with which Aristotle had associated it, and to strive toward the unelaborated, the "pre-semiological" (Barthes), the "unstructured" (Mukařovský).[50] Since about the middle of the nineteenth century, in Barthes' view, literature has been engaged in a tireless struggle to halt the appropriation of language by myth and to break down the parasitic secondary systems of meaning which threaten creative culture with strangulation. Thus the wheel has turned full circle and the relative positions of history and poetry, as Aristotle perceived them, have been reversed.[51]

Many modern historians, as we have seen, have repudiated the goals and premises of historical realism, and certain aspects of the rhetoric of the old historical realism have in fact disappeared from modern historical texts. But there seems to have been no radical reform of the historian's mode of writing comparable with the changes that have affected literary writing and fiction in the last half-century. Historical texts continue to recount calmly events and situations located in the past as though the "age of suspicion" had never dawned. In the remarkable Preface to *La Méditerranée,* Fernand Braudel acknowledges that there is a subject of the enunciation of the historical

49. Ibid., p. 37.

50. On Jan Mukařovský's categories of normative or structured and functional or unstructured, see the essay "The Esthetics of Language" (orig. pub. in *Slovo a Slovesnost* [1940], 6:1–27), in *A Prague School Reader on Esthetics, Literary Structure, and Style,* selected and trans. Paul N. Garvin (Washington: Georgetown Univ. Press, 1964), pp. 31–69.

51. It is important to emphasize that Barthes' argument does not rest on a radical opposition between "natural" meaning (authenticity) and the signs of culture (inauthenticity). Barthes makes it clear that both poetry and history are semiological systems. There is no nature, no outside of signs and the act of signifying. The question is whether the signifying system attempts to cover up its tracks so as to appear natural, or whether, on the contrary, in the forlorn yet utopian hope of breaking out of its own constraints, it tests itself to the very limit; whether, in other terms, it is integrationist and thus fundamentally conservative, or disruptive and revolutionary. Although he shares many common positions with Sartrian existentialism in this essay, Barthes' interpretation of the "essentialist" aspirations of poetry is quite different from Sartre's.

account, but the signs of this subject are erased from the main body of Braudel's text. Of the historical writings I know, the one that comes closest to breaking the historical code is perhaps Michelet's *La Sorcière*, which appeared over one hundred years ago. Yet the historians who have recuperated Michelet from the domain of literature, to which he had been banished by their Positivist predecessors, have been attentive above all to the range of questions he asked of the past, to his acute sense of the richness of historical phenomena. They have hardly commented at all on the peculiar features of a text of unusual density and complexity, in which the account of events is so shot through with lyrical and confessional writing, and fiction is so intimately interwoven with traditional historical narrative, that the reader is disoriented and made uncertain as to what is history and what is dream or poetic effusion, what is a narrative of past events (*histoire*) and what belongs to the situation at the time of writing or enunciating and to the subject of the enunciation (*discours*).[52] It is as though Michelet were stretching to the limit the distinctions between subject and object, fact and fiction, present and past, *énonciation* and *énoncé*, *discours* and *histoire*. It is this disturbing feature—disturbing even today—of Michelet's writing that historians neither comment upon nor, apparently, wish to emulate.

In literature, on the other hand, attempts to push outward the limits of language have become the central focus of the writer's activity. In Barthes' words, "The writer [*écrivain*]—and in this respect he stands alone, apart from, and in opposition to all speakers and mere practitioners of writing [*écrivants*]—is he who refuses to let the obligations of his language speak for him, who knows and is acutely conscious of the deficiencies of his idiom, and who imagines, utopically, a total language in which *nothing* is obligatory."[53] Not surprisingly, several contemporary "novelists" are probing the very distinction of *histoire* and *discours* on which, as we saw, classical narrative (including, naturally, classical historical narrative) rests. In Sollers' novel *Drame*, Barthes writes,

> we are placed in the presence not of something narrated but of the labor of narration. This thin line separating the product from its creation, the

52. In his introduction to a recent edition of *La Sorcière* (Paris: Julliard, 1964), Robert Mandrou, for instance, manages to say nothing of the text itself, passing instead immediately through it, as it were, to what in his view it represents—a Weberian ideal type of the witch. *La Sorcière* is thus reappropriated for history by placing in parentheses those aspects of it which, to the literary scholar, are most striking and specific. No doubt it would be more easily assimilated if it could be rewritten as a Weberian text.

53. "Drame, poème, roman," in *Théorie d'ensemble*, p. 37, n. 7.

narrative-as-object from the narrative-as-labor, is the historical divide
that sets the classical tale, which emerges completely armed from a prior
labor of preparation, over against the modern text, which has no desire
to exist prior to its enunciation and which, presenting its own labor to be
read, can only be read, in the end, as labor. . . . The classical narrator
sets himself up in front of us, as one says "to sit down to table" (even in
the special sense in which this expression is used in the language of
crime) [*se mettre à table* = to confess, to "come clean"] and exhibits his
wares (his soul, his learning, his memories); to this position corresponds,
in punctuation, the fatidical colon of the exordium that is poised, ready
to top itself off with a fine tale. The narrator of *Drame* has erased the
colon and given up all idea of setting himself up.

Similarly, the time of this "novel" is no longer marked by the two
axes of the time of the narrative and the time of the narration, the
imagined time of the story (*axe de fiction*) and the very time of the
succession of the words of the text (*axe de notation*).

The axis of notation absorbs all temporality: there is no time outside the
Book: the scenes that are related (and we can never tell, for good
reason, if they are dreams, memories, or fantasies) do not imply any
fictitious frame of reference which would be "other" than their situation on the page. The notational axis is absolutely the only one. A
writer could indeed reject all narrative chronology and yet subordinate
his notation to the flux of his impressions, memories, sensations, etc.,
but that would still be to maintain the two axes, making the notational
one a copy of *another* temporality. That, however, is not the technique
of *Drame;* there is literally no time here, other than that of the words.
What we have is an undivided present, which is that of the subject only
to the extent that the latter is entirely absorbed by his function as
narrator, that is to say, spinner of words.[54]

In Voltaire's or Gibbon's time, as in that of Thierry or Macaulay,
the work of the literary artist and that of the historian were intimately
connected, even, as I have tried to argue, indistinguishable. Voltaire
was at one and the same time a writer, as we say, and a historian, and
Gibbon and Hume both considered themselves men of letters. Literature, by Hume's own account, was "the ruling passion of my life and
the great source of my enjoyment." Thierry and his friends were
closely attentive to the work of contemporary novelists and the latter
returned the compliment. It is not fortuitous that Scott was a key
figure for both Thierry and Balzac, or that Thierry and Manzoni followed each other's work carefully. Modern history and modern literature have both rejected the ideal of representation that dominated

54. Ibid., p. 36.

them for so long. Both now conceive of their work as exploration, testing, creation of new meanings, rather than as disclosure or revelation of meanings already in some sense "there," but not immediately perceptible. In the course of this change of orientation, however, literature has come to be increasingly preoccupied with language as the instrument of meaning, whereas history may well dream of escaping from ordinary or natural language to the highly formal languages of the sciences. As a result, it is not easy for us today to see who is, as a *writer,* the Joyce or the Kafka of modern historiography in the way that Gibbon could be viewed as its Fielding, Thierry as its Balzac, Michelet as its Hugo.

Moreover, many historians cling to a notion of writing or of literary style that is remote from the modern writer's conception of his art. Stressing the value of clarity and elegance, a distinguished historian recently reaffirmed the ornamental and rhetorical function of literary style in the writing of history. The function of style, it is said, is to capture and hold the reader's attention, to convey ideas as effectively as possible, and, in the end, to confirm the pact that unites writer and reader in a common universe of meanings. "Unless the substance is good, the appearance, painted even an inch thick, will not please." As the aim of literary style is to ensure "readability," and the historian's primary concern as a writer is to secure his audience, "books should differ with the people to whom they are addressed." The historian writes for an audience that already accepts his terms and that shares his basic values and assumptions. "Regard your audience as intelligent though possibly uninstructed. . . . No problem of historical study that I have come across, has seemed to me incapable of being explained with full clarity to any person of reasonable intelligence, and no person of insufficient intelligence will anyhow be in the way of reading or hearing historical analysis and description."[55] For the historian, in sum, rhetorical rather than poetic considerations remain paramount, and literature is still a craft or skill by which the *dulce* can be joined to the *utile* and the friendly reader delighted even as he is instructed. Literary artists and historians are apparently much further apart both in their conception and in their practice of literature than they have been in the past. Indeed, the historian who conceives of literature in this way—as "style" or as a means of adorning otherwise simple propositions—may bring history close to Literature (in Barthes' designation): but he will be further than ever from the concerns of the contemporary literary artist.

55. G. R. Elton, *The Practice of History* (Sydney, Australia: Sydney Univ. Press, 1967), pp. 109, 115, 116.

Hayden White

2
THE HISTORICAL TEXT
AS LITERARY ARTIFACT

One of the ways that a scholarly field takes stock of itself is by considering its history. Yet it is difficult to get an objective history of a scholarly discipline, because, if the historian is himself a practitioner of it, he is likely to be a devotee of one or another of its sects and hence biased, and if he is not a practitioner, he is unlikely to have the expertise necessary to distinguish between the significant and the insignificant events of his field's development. One might think that these difficulties would not arise in the field of history itself, but they do, and not only for the reasons mentioned above. In order to write the history of any given scholarly discipline or even of a science, one must be prepared to ask questions about it of a sort that do not have to be asked in the practice of it. One must try to get behind or beneath the presuppositions that sustain a given type of inquiry and ask the questions that can be begged in its practice in the interest of determining why this type of inquiry has been designed to solve the problems it characteristically tries to solve. This is what metahistory seeks to do. It addresses itself to such questions as: What is the structure of a peculiarly historical consciousness? What is the epistemological status of historical explanations as compared with other kinds of explanations that might be offered to account for the materials with which historians ordinarily deal? What are the possible forms of historical representation and what are their bases? By what authority can historical accounts claim to be contributions to a secured knowledge of reality in general and to the human sciences in particular?

Many of these questions have been dealt with quite competently over the last quarter-century by philosophers concerned to define

This essay is a revised version of a lecture given before the Comparative Literature Colloquium of Yale University in January 1974. In it I have tried to elaborate some of the themes that I originally discussed in an article, "The Structure of Historical Narrative," *Clio*, 1 (1972), 5–20. I have also drawn upon the materials of my book *Metahistory: The Historical Imagination in Nineteenth-Century Europe* (Baltimore: Johns Hopkins Univ. Press, 1973), especially the introduction, titled "The Poetics of History." The essay profited from conversations with Michael Holquist and Geoffrey Hartman, both of Yale University and both experts in the theory of narrative.

history's relationships to other disciplines, especially the physical and social sciences, and by historians interested in assessing the success of their discipline in mapping the past and determining the relationship of that past to the present. But there is one problem that neither philosophers nor historians have looked at very seriously and to which literary theorists have given only passing attention. This question has to do with the status of the historical narrative considered purely as a verbal artifact that purports to be a model of structures and processes that are long past and cannot therefore be subjected to either experimental or observational controls. This is not to say that historians and philosophers of history have failed to take notice of the essentially provisional and contingent nature of historical representations and of their susceptibility to infinite revision in the light of new evidence or more sophisticated conceptualizations of problems. One of the marks of a good professional historian is the consistency with which he reminds his readers of the purely provisional nature of his characterizations of events, agents, and agencies found in the always incomplete historical record. Nor is it to say that literary theorists have never studied the structure of historical narratives. But in general there has been a reluctance to consider historical narratives as what they most manifestly are—verbal fictions, the contents of which are as much invented as found and the forms of which have more in common with their counterparts in literature than they have with those in the sciences.

The evasion of the implications of the fictive nature of historical narrative is in part a consequence of the utility of the concept "history" for the definition of other types of discourse. "History" can be set over against "science" by virtue of its want of conceptual rigor and failure to produce the kinds of universal laws that the sciences characteristically seek to produce. Similarly, "history" can be set over against "literature" by virtue of its interest in the "actual" rather than the "possible," which is supposedly the object of representation of literary works. Thus, within a long and distinguished critical tradition that has sought to determine what is "real" and what is "imagined" in the novel, history has served as a kind of archetype of the realistic pole of representation. I am thinking of Northrop Frye, Erich Auerbach, Wayne Booth, Robert Scholes and Robert Kellogg, and others. Nor is it unusual for literary theorists, when they are speaking about the "context" of a literary work, to suppose that this context, the "historical milieu," has a concreteness and an accessibility that the work itself can never have, as if it were easier to perceive the reality of a past world put together from a thousand historical documents than it is to probe the depths of a single literary work that is present to the critic studying it. But the presumed concreteness and accessibility of historical milieus, these contexts of the texts that literary scholars study, are themselves products of the fictive capability of the historians who have studied those contexts. The historical documents are not less opaque than the texts studied by the literary critic. Nor is the world those documents figure more accessible. The one is no more "given" than the other. In fact, the opaqueness of the world figured in historical documents is, if anything, increased by the production of historical narratives. Each new historical work only adds to the number of possible texts that have to be interpreted if a full and accurate picture of a given historical milieu is to be faithfully drawn. The relationship between the past to be analyzed and historical works produced by analysis of the documents is paradoxical; the more we know about the past, the more difficult it is to generalize about it.

But if the increase in our knowledge of the past makes it more difficult to generalize about it, it should make it easier for us to generalize about the forms in which that knowledge is transmitted to us. Our knowledge of the past may increase incrementally, but our understanding of it does not. Nor does our understanding of the past progress by the kind of revolutionary breakthroughs that we associate with the development of the physical sciences. Like literature, history progresses by the production of classics, the nature of which is such that they cannot be disconfirmed or negated in the way that the principal conceptual schemata of the sciences are. And it is their non-disconfirmability that testifies to the essentially literary nature of historical classics. There is something in a historical masterpiece that cannot be negated, and this non-negatable element is its form, the form which is its fiction.

It is frequently forgotten or, when remembered, denied, that no given set of events attested by the historical record constitutes a story manifestly finished and complete. This is as true of the events that constitute the life of an individual as it is of an institution, a nation, or a whole people. We do not live stories, even if we give our lives meaning by retrospectively casting them in the form of stories. And so too with nations or whole cultures. In an essay on the "mythical" nature of historiography, Lévi-Strauss remarks on the astonishment that a visitor from another planet would feel if confronted by the thousands of histories actually written about the French Revolution. For in those works, the "authors do not always make use of the same incidents; when they do, the incidents are revealed in different lights.

And yet these are variations which have to do with the same country, the same period, and the same events—events whose reality is scattered across every level of a multilayered structure." He goes on to suggest that the criterion of validity by which historical accounts might be assessed cannot depend on their "elements," that is to say their putative "factual" content. On the contrary, he notes, "Pursued in isolation, each element shows itself to be beyond grasp. But certain of them derive consistency from the fact that they can be integrated into a system whose terms are more or less credible when set against the overall coherence of the series." But this coherence of the series cannot be the coherence of the chronological series, that sequence of "facts" organized into the temporal order of their original occurrence. For the "chronicle" of events, out of which the historian fashions his story of "what really happened," already comes pre-encoded. There are "hot" and "cold" chronologies, chronologies in which more or less numbers of dates appear to demand inclusion in a full "chronicle" of "what happened." Moreover, the "dates" themselves come to us already grouped into "classes of dates," classes which constitute putative "domains" of the historical field, domains which appear as problems for the historian to solve if he is to give a full and culturally responsible account of the past.[1]

All this suggests to Lévi-Strauss that, when it is a matter of working up a comprehensive account of the various domains of the historical record in the form of a story, the "alleged historical continuities" that the historian purports to find in the record are "secured only by dint of fraudulent outlines" imposed by the historian on the record. These fraudulent outlines are, in his view, a product of "abstraction" and a means of escape from the "threat of an infinite regress" that always lurks at the interior of the very complex of historical "facts." We can construct a comprehensible story of the past, Lévi-Strauss insists, only by a decision to "give up" one or more of the domains of facts offering themselves for inclusion in our accounts. Our explanations of historical structures and processes are thus determined more by what we leave out of our representations than by what we put in. For it is in this brutal capacity to exclude certain facts in the interest of constituting others as components of comprehensible stories that the historian displays his tact as well as his understanding. The "overall coherence" of any given "series" of historical facts is the coherence of story, but this coherence is achieved only by a tailoring

1. Claude Lévi-Strauss, "Overture to *le Cru et le cuit*," trans. Joseph H. McMahon, *Yale French Studies,* Nos. 36–37 (1966), pp. 56–59; and *The Savage Mind* (London: Weidenfeld and Nicolson, 1962), pp. 258–63.

of the "facts" to the requirements of the story form. And thus Lévi-Strauss concludes: "In spite of worthy and indispensable efforts to bring another moment in history alive and to possess it, a clairvoyant history should admit that it never completely escapes from the nature of myth."[2]

It is obvious that this conflation of mythic and historical consciousness will offend some historians and disturb those literary theorists whose conception of literature presupposes a radical opposition of history to fiction or of fact to fancy. As Frye has remarked: "In a sense the historical is the opposite of the mythical, and to tell the historian that what gives shape to his book is a myth would sound to him vaguely insulting." Yet Frye himself grants that "when a historian's scheme gets to a certain point of comprehensiveness it becomes mythical in shape, and so approaches the poetic in its structure." He even speaks of different kinds of historical myths: romantic myths "based on a quest or pilgrimage to a City of God or classless society"; comic "myths of progress through evolution or revolution"; tragic myths of "decline and fall, like the works of Gibbon and Spengler"; and ironic "myths of recurrence or casual catastrophe." But Frye appears to believe that these myths are operative only in such victims of what might be called the "poetic fallacy" as Hegel, Marx, Nietzsche, Spengler, Toynbee, and Sartre—historians whose fascination with the "constructive" capacity of human thought has deadened their responsibility to the "found" data. "The historian works inductively," he says, "collecting his facts and trying to avoid any informing patterns except those he sees, or is honestly convinced he sees, in the facts themselves." He does not work "from" a "unifying form," as the poet does, but "toward" it; and it therefore follows that the historian, like any writer of discursive prose, is to be judged "by the truth of what he says, or by the adequacy of his verbal reproduction of his external model," whether that external model be the actions of past men or the historian's own thought about such actions.[3]

What Frye says is true enough as a statement of the ideal that has inspired historical writing since the time of the Greeks, but that ideal presupposes an opposition between myth and history that is as problematical as it is venerable. It serves Frye's purposes very well, since it permits him to locate the specifically "fictive" in the space between the two concepts of the "mythic" and the "historical." As readers of

2. "Overture," p. 57.
3. Northrop Frye, "New Directions from Old," in *Fables of Identity* (New York: Harcourt, Brace & World, 1963), pp. 52–58.

Frye's *Anatomy of Criticism* will remember, Frye conceives fictions to consist in part of sublimates of archetypal myth-structures. These structures have been displaced to the interior of verbal artifacts in such a way as to serve as their latent meanings. The fundamental meanings of all fictions, their thematic content, consist, in Frye's view, of the "pre-generic plot-structures" or "mythoi" derived from the corpora of classical and Judaeo-Christian religious literature. According to this theory, we understand why a particular story has "turned out" as it has when we have identified the archetypal myth, or pre-generic plot-structure, of which the story is an exemplification. And we see the "point" of a story when we have identified its theme (Frye's translation of *dianoia*), which makes of it a "parable or illustrative fable." "Every work of literature," Frye insists, "has both a fictional and a thematic aspect," but as we move from "fictional projection" toward the overt articulation of theme, the writing tends to take on the aspect of "direct address, or straight discursive writing and cease[s] to be literature." And in Frye's view, as we have seen, history (or at least "proper history") belongs to the category of "discursive writing," so that when the fictional element—or mythic plot-structure—is obviously present in it, it ceases to be history altogether and becomes a bastard genre, the product of an unholy, though not unnatural, union between history and poetry.

Yet, I would argue, histories gain part of their explanatory effect by their success in making stories out of mere chronicles; and stories in turn are made out of chronicles by an operation that I have elsewhere called "emplotment." By emplotment I mean simply the encodation of the facts contained in the chronicle as components of specific kinds of plot-structures, in precisely the way that Frye has suggested is the case with "fictions" in general.

The late R. G. Collingwood insisted that the historian was above all a storyteller and suggested that historical sensibility was manifested in the capacity to make a plausible story out of a congeries of "facts" which, in their unprocessed form, made no sense at all. In their efforts to make sense of the historical record, which is fragmentary and always incomplete, historians have to make use of what Collingwood called "the constructive imagination," which told the historian—as it tells the competent detective—what "must have been the case" given the available evidence and the formal properties it displayed to the consciousness capable of putting the right question to it. This constructive imagination functions in much the same way that Kant supposed the a priori imagination functions when it tells us that, even though we cannot perceive both sides of a tabletop simultaneously, we can be certain it has two sides if it has one, because the very concept of one side entails at least one other. Collingwood suggested that historians come to their evidence endowed with a sense of the possible forms that different kinds of recognizably human situations can take. He called this sense the nose for the "story" contained in the evidence or for the "true" story that was buried in or hidden behind the "apparent" story. And he concluded that historians provide plausible explanations for bodies of historical evidence when they succeed in discovering the "story" or complex of "stories" implicitly contained within them.[4]

What Collingwood failed to see was that no given set of casually recorded historical events in themselves constitute a story; the most that they offer to the historian are story elements. The events are made into a story by the suppression or subordination of certain of them and the highlighting of others, by characterization, motific repetition, variation of tone and point of view, alternative descriptive strategies, and the like—in short, all of the techniques that we would normally expect to find in the emplotment of a novel or a play. For example, no historical event is intrinsically tragic; it can only be conceived as such from a particular point of view or from within the context of a structured set of events of which it is an element enjoying a privileged place. For in history what is tragic from one perspective is comic from another, just as in society what appears to be "tragic" from the standpoint of one class may be, as Marx purported to show in the *Eighteenth Brumaire of Louis Bonaparte,* only a "farce" from that of another class. Considered as potential elements of a story, historical events are value-neutral. Whether they find their place finally in a story that is tragic, comic, romantic or ironic—to use Frye's categories—depends upon the historian's decision to configure them according to the imperatives of one plot-structure or mythos rather than another. The same set of events can serve as components of a story that is tragic or comic, as the case may be, depending on the historian's choice of the plot-structure that he considers most appropriate for ordering events of that kind so as to make them into a comprehensible story.

This suggests that what the historian brings to his consideration of the historical record is a notion of the types of configurations of events that can be recognized as stories by the audience for which he is writing. True, his story can misfire. I do not suppose that anyone

4. R. G. Collingwood, *The Idea of History* (Oxford: Clarendon, 1946; rpt. New York: Oxford Univ. Press, 1956), pp. 231–49.

would accept the emplotment of the life of President Kennedy as comedy, but whether it ought to be emplotted romantically, tragically, or satirically is an open question. The important point is that most historical sequences can be emplotted in a number of different ways so as to provide different interpretations of those events and to endow them with different meanings. Thus, for example, what Michelet in his great history of the French Revolution construed as a drama of Romantic transcendence, his contemporary Tocqueville emplotted as an ironic tragedy. Neither can be said to have had more knowledge of the "facts" contained in the record; they simply had different notions of the kind of story that best fitted the facts they knew. Nor should it be thought that they told different stories of the Revolution because they had discovered different kinds of facts, political on the one hand, social on the other. They sought out different kinds of facts because they had different kinds of stories to tell. But why did these alternative, not to say mutually exclusive, representations of what was substantially the same set of events appear equally plausible to their respective audiences? Simply because the historians shared with their audiences certain preconceptions about how the Revolution might be emplotted, in response to imperatives that were generally extrahistorical, ideological, aesthetic, or mythical, in nature.

Collingwood once remarked that you could never explicate a tragedy to anyone who was not already acquainted with the kinds of situations that are regarded as "tragic" in our culture. Anyone who has taught or taken one of those omnibus courses, usually entitled Western Civilization or Introduction to the Classics of Western Literature, will know what Collingwood had in mind. Unless you have some idea of the generic attributes of tragic, comic, romantic, or ironic situations, you will be unable to recognize them as such when you come upon them in a literary text. But historical situations do not have built into them intrinsic meanings in the way that literary texts do. Historical situations are not inherently tragic, comic, or romantic. They may all be inherently ironic, but they need not be emplotted that way. All the historian needs to do to transform a tragic into a comic situation is to shift his point of view or change the scope of his perceptions. In any case, we only think of situations as tragic or comic because these concepts are part of our generally cultural and specifically literary heritage. How a given historical situation is to be configured depends on the historian's subtlety in matching up a specific plot-structure with the set of historical events that he wishes to endow with a meaning of a particular kind. This is essentially a literary, that is to say fiction-making, operation. And to call it that in no way detracts from the status of historical narratives as providing a kind of knowledge. For not only are the pregeneric plot-structures by which sets of events can be constituted as stories of a particular kind limited in number, as Frye and other archetypal critics suggest; but the encodation of events in terms of such plot-structures is one of the ways that a culture has of making sense of both personal and public pasts.

We can make sense of sets of events in a number of different ways. One of the ways is to subsume the events under the causal laws that may have governed their concatenation in order to produce the particular configuration that the events appear to assume when considered as "effects" of mechanical forces. This is the way of scientific explanation. Another way we make sense of a set of events that appears strange, enigmatic, or mysterious in its immediate manifestations is to encode the set in terms of culturally provided categories, such as metaphysical concepts, religious beliefs, or story forms. The effect of such encodation is to familiarize the unfamiliar, and in general this is the way of historiography, whose "data" are always immediately strange, not to say exotic, simply by virtue of their distance from us in time and their origination in a way of life different from our own.

The historian shares with his audience general notions of the forms that significant human situations must take by virtue of his participation in the specific processes of sense-making that identify him as a member of one cultural endowment rather than another. In the process of studying a given complex of events, he begins to perceive the possible story form that such events may figure. In his narrative account of how this set of events took on the shape that he perceives to inhere within it, he emplots his account as a story of a particular kind. The reader, in the process of following the historian's account of those events, gradually comes to realize that the story he is reading is of one kind rather than another: romance, tragedy, comedy, satire, epic, or what have you. And when he has perceived the class or type of stories to which the story that he is reading belongs, he experiences the effect of having the events in the story explained to him. He has at this point not only successfully followed the story, he has grasped the point of it, understood it, as well. The original strangeness, mystery, or exoticism of the events is dispelled and they take on a familiar aspect, not in their details, but in their functions as elements of a familiar kind of configuration. They are rendered comprehensible by being subsumed under the categories of the plot-structure in which they are encoded as a story of a particular kind. They are familiarized, not only because the reader now has more information about the events, but also because he has been shown how the data conform to an icon of a comprehensible finished process, a plot-structure with which he is familiar as a part of his cultural endowment.

This is not unlike what happens, or is supposed to happen, in psychotherapy. The set of events in the patient's past that is the presumed cause of his distress, manifested in the neurotic syndrome, has been defamiliarized, rendered strange, mysterious, and threatening and assumed a meaning that he can neither accept nor effectively reject. It is not that the patient does not know what those events were, does not know the facts; for if he did not in some sense know the facts, he would be unable to recognize them and repress them whenever they arise in his consciousness. On the contrary, he knows them all too well. He knows them so well, in fact, that he lives with them constantly and in such a way as to make it impossible for him to see any other facts except through the coloration that the set of events in question gives to his perception of the world. We might say that, according to the theory of psychoanalysis, the patient has over-emplotted these events, has charged them with a meaning so intense that, whether real or merely imagined, they continue to shape both his perceptions and his responses to the world long after they should have become "past history." The therapist's problem, then, is not to hold up before the patient the "real facts" of the matter, the "truth" as against the "fantasy" that obsesses him. Nor is it to give him a short course in psychoanalytical theory by which to enlighten him as to the true nature of his distress by cataloging it as a manifestation of some "complex." This is what the analyst might do in relating the patient's case to a third party, and especially to another analyst. But psychoanalytic theory recognizes that the patient will resist both of these tactics in the same way that he resists the intrusion into consciousness of the traumatized memory traces in the form that he obsessively remembers them. The problem is to get the patient to re-emplot his whole life history in such a way as to change the meaning of those events for him and their significance for the economy of the whole set of events that make up his life. As thus envisaged, the therapeutic process is an exercise in the refamiliarization of events that have been defamiliarized, rendered alienated from the patient's life history, by virtue of their overdetermination as causal forces. And we might say that the events are detraumatized by being removed from the plot-structure in which they have a dominant place and inserted in another in which they have a subordinate or simply ordinary function as elements of a life shared with all other men.

I am not interested in forcing the analogy between psychotherapy and historiography; I use the example merely to illustrate a point about the fictive component in historical narratives. Historians seek to refamiliarize us with events that have been forgotten through either accident, neglect, or repression. Moreover, the greatest historians have always dealt with those events in the histories of their cultures that are "traumatic" in nature and the meaning of which is either problematical or overdetermined in the significance that they still have for current life—events such as revolutions, civil wars, large-scale processes such as industrialization and urbanization, or institutions that have lost their original function in a society but continue to play an important role on the current social scene. In looking at the ways in which such structures took shape or evolved, historians refamiliarize them not only by providing more information about them, but also by showing how their developments conformed to one or another of the story types that we conventionally invoke to make sense of our own life histories.

If any of this is plausible as a characterization of the explanatory effect of historical narrative, it tells us something important about the mimetic aspect of historical narratives. It is generally maintained, as Frye stated, that a history is a verbal model of a set of events external to the mind of the historian. But it is wrong to think of a history as a model similar to a scale model of an airplane or ship, or a map or photograph. For with a photograph we can check its adequacy by looking at the original and, by applying the necessary rules of translation, seeing in what respect the model has actually succeeded in reproducing aspects of the original. But historical structures and processes are not like these originals; we cannot look at them to see if the historian has adequately reproduced them in his narrative. Nor should we want to, even if we could; for after all it was the very strangeness of the original as it appeared in the documents that inspired the historian's efforts to make a model of it in the first place. If the historian only did that for us we should be in the same situation as the patient whose analyst merely told him, on the basis of interviews with his parents, siblings, and childhood friends, what the "true facts" of the patient's early life were. We would have no reason to think that anything at all had been explained to us.

This is what leads me to think that historical narratives are not only models of past events and processes, but also metaphorical statements which suggest a relation of similitude between such events and processes and the story types that we conventionally use to endow the events of our lives with culturally sanctioned meanings. Viewed in a purely formal way, a historical narrative is not only a reproduction of the events reported in it, it is also a complex of symbols that gives us directions for finding an icon of the structure of those events in our literary tradition.

I am here of course invoking the distinctions between sign, symbol, and icon that C. S. Peirce developed in his philosophy of language. I think that these distinctions will help us to understand what is fictive in all putatively realistic representations of the world and what is realistic in all manifestly fictive ones. They help us, in short, to answer the question, What are historical representations representations of? It seems to me that we must say of histories what Frye seems to think is true only of poetry or philosophies of history, namely that, considered as a system of signs, the historical narrative points in two directions simultaneously: toward the events described in the narrative and toward the story type or mythos that the historian has chosen to serve as the icon of the structure of the events. The narrative itself is not the icon; what it does is describe events in the historical record in such a way as to inform the reader what to take as an icon of the events so as to render them "familiar" to him. The historical narrative thus mediates between the events reported in it and the generic plot-structures conventionally used in our culture to endow unfamiliar events and situations with meanings.

It is this mediative function that permits us to speak of a historical narrative as an extended metaphor. As a symbolic structure, the historical narrative does not reproduce the events it describes; it tells us in what direction to think about the events and charges our thought about the events with different emotional valences. The historical narrative does not image the things it indicates; it calls to mind images of the things it indicates, in the same way that a metaphor does. When a given course of events is emplotted as a "tragedy," this simply means that the historian has so described the events as to remind us of that form of fiction which we associate with the concept "tragic." Properly understood, histories ought never to be read as unambiguous signs of the events they report, but rather as symbolic structures, extended metaphors, that "liken" the events reported in them to some form with which we have already become familiar in our literary culture.

Perhaps I should indicate briefly what is meant by the symbolic and iconic aspects of a metaphor. The hackneyed phrase "my love, a rose" is not, obviously, intended to be understood as suggesting that the loved one is actually a rose. It is not even meant to suggest that the loved one has the specific attributes of a rose, that is to say, that the loved one is red, yellow, orange or black, is a plant, has thorns, needs sunlight, should be sprayed regularly with insecticides, and so on. It is meant to be understood as indicating that the beloved shares the qualities which the rose has come to symbolize in the customary linguistic usages of Western culture. That is to say, considered as a message, the metaphor gives directions for finding an entity that will evoke the images associated with loved ones and roses alike in our culture. The metaphor does not image the thing it seeks to characterize, it gives directions for finding the set of images that are intended to be associated with that thing. It functions as a symbol rather than as a sign, which is to say that it does not give us either a description or an icon of the thing it represents, but tells us what images to look for in our culturally encoded experience in order to determine how we should feel about the thing represented.[5]

So too for historical narratives. They succeed in endowing sets of past events with meanings over and above whatever comprehension they provide by appeal to putative causal laws, by exploiting the metaphorical similarities between sets of real events and the conventional structures of our fictions. By the very constitution of a set of events in such a way as to make a comprehensible story out of them, the historian charges those events with the symbolic significance of a comprehensible plot-structure. Historians may not like to think of their works as translations of "fact" into "fiction"; but this is one of the effects of their works. By suggesting alternative emplotments of a given sequence of historical events, historians provide historical events with all of the possible meanings with which the literary art of their culture is capable of endowing them. The real dispute between the "proper historian" and the "philosopher of history" has to do with the latter's insistence that events can be emplotted in one and only one story form. History writing thrives on the discovery of all the possible plot-structures that might be invoked to endow sets of events with different meanings. And our understanding of the past increases precisely in the degree to which we succeed in determining how far that past conforms to the strategies of sense-making that are contained in their purest forms in literary art.

Conceiving historical narratives in this way may give us some insight into the crisis in historical thinking that has been under way since the beginning of our century. Imagine that the problem of the historian is to make sense of a hypothetical set of events by arranging

5. See Paul Henle, ed., *Language, Thought, and Culture* (Ann Arbor: Univ. of Michigan Press, 1966), pp. 173–96.

them in a series that is at once chronologically and syntactically structured, in the way that any discourse from a sentence all the way up to
a novel is structured. We can see immediately that the imperatives of
chronological arrangement of the events constituting the set must
exist in tension with the imperatives of the syntactical strategies al-
luded to whether the latter are conceived as those of logic (the syllo-
gism) or those of narrative (the plot-structure).

Thus, we have a set of events

$$1.\ a,\ b,\ c,\ d,\ e,\ \ldots,\ n$$

ordered chronologically but requiring description and characterization
as elements of plot or argument by which to give them meaning. The
series can be emplotted in a number of different ways and thereby
endowed with different meanings without violating the imperatives of
the chronological arrangement at all. We may briefly characterize
some of these emplotments in the following way.

$$2.\ A,\ b,\ c,\ d,\ e,\ \ldots,\ n$$
$$3.\ a,\ B,\ c,\ d,\ e,\ \ldots,\ n$$
$$4.\ a,\ b,\ C,\ d,\ e,\ \ldots,\ n$$
$$5.\ a,\ b,\ c,\ D,\ e,\ \ldots,\ n$$

And so on.

The capitalized letters indicate the privileged status given to certain
events or sets of events in the series by which they are endowed with
explanatory force, either as causes explaining the structure of the
whole series or as symbols of the plot-structure of the series considered as a story of a specific kind. We might say that any history
that endows any putatively "original" event (a) with the status of a
decisive factor (A) in the structuration of the whole series of events
following after it is "deterministic." The emplotments of the history
of "society" by Rousseau in his *Discourse on the Origin of Inequal-
ity,* Marx in the *Manifesto,* and Freud in *Totem and Taboo* would fall
into this category. So too any history that endows the last event in the
series (e), whether real or only speculatively projected, with the force
of full explanatory power (E) is of the type of all eschatological or
apocalyptical histories. St. Augustine's *City of God* and the various
versions of the Joachimte notion of the advent of a final era, Hegel's
Philosophy of History, and in general all Idealist histories are of this
sort. In between we would have the various forms of historiography
that appeal to plot-structures of a distinctively "fictional" sort (romance, comedy, tragedy, and satire) by which to endow the series
with a perceivable form and a conceivable "meaning."

If the series was simply recorded in the order in which the events originally occurred, under the assumption that the ordering of the events in their temporal sequence itself provided a kind of explanation of why they occurred when and where they did, we would have the pure form of the chronicle. This would be a "naïve" form of chronicle, however, inasmuch as the categories of time and space alone served as the informing interpretative principles. Over against the naïve form of chronicle we could postulate as a logical possibility its "sentimental" counterpart, the ironic denial that historical series have any kind of larger significance or describe any imaginable plot-structure or indeed can even be construed as a story with a discernible beginning, middle, and end. We could conceive of such accounts of history as intended to serve as antidotes to their "false" or "over-emplotted" counterparts (nos. 2, 3, 4 and 5 above) and could represent them as an ironic return to chronicle as a way of constituting the only sense that a cognitively responsible history could take. We could characterize such histories as

6. "$a, b, c, d, e, \ldots, n$"

with the quotation marks indicating the conscious interpretation of the events as having nothing other than seriality as their meaning.

This schema is of course highly abstract and does not do justice to the possible mixtures of and variations within the types that it is meant to distinguish. But it helps us, I think, to conceive how events might be emplotted in different ways without violating the imperatives of the chronological order of the events (however they are construed) so as to yield alternative, mutually exclusive, and yet equally plausible interpretations of the set. I have tried to show in *Metahistory* how such mixtures and variations occur in the writings of the master historians of the nineteenth century, and I have suggested in that book that classic historical accounts always represent attempts both to emplot the historical series adequately and implicitly to come to terms with other plausible emplotments. It is this dialectical tension between two or more possible emplotments that signals the element of critical self-consciousness present in any historian of recognizably classic stature.

Histories, then, are not only about events but also about the possible sets of relationships that those events can be demonstrated to figure. These sets of relationships are not, however, immanent in the events themselves; they exist only in the mind of the historian reflecting on them. Here they are present as the modes of relationships conceptualized in the myth, fable, and folklore, the scientific knowledge, religion, and literary art of the historian's own culture.

But more important, they are—I suggest—immanent in the very language which the historian must use to describe events prior to a scientific analysis of them or a ficitional emplotment of them. For if the historian's aim is to familiarize us with the unfamiliar, he must use figurative, rather than technical, language. Technical languages are familiarizing only to those who have been indoctrinated in their uses and only of those sets of events that the practitioners of a discipline have agreed to describe in a uniform terminology. History possesses no such generally accepted technical terminology and in fact no agreement on what kinds of events make up its specific subject matter. The historian's characteristic instrument of encodation, communication, and exchange is ordinary educated speech. This implies that the only instruments that he has for endowing his data with meaning, of rendering the strange familiar, and of rendering the mysterious past comprehensible, are the techniques of figurative language. All historical narratives presuppose figurative characterizations of the events they purport to represent and explain. And this means that historical narratives, considered purely as verbal artifacts, can be characterized by the mode of figurative discourse in which they are cast.

If this is the case, then it may well be that the kind of emplotment that the historian decides to use to give meaning to a set of historical events is dictated by the dominant figurative mode of the language he has used to describe the elements of his account prior to his composition of a narrative. Geoffrey Hartman once remarked that he was not sure that he knew what historians of literature might want to do, but he did know that to write a history meant to place an event within a context by relating it as a part to some conceivable whole. He went on to suggest that as far as he knew, there were only two ways of relating parts to wholes, by metonymy and by synecdoche. Having been engaged for some time in the study of the thought of Giambattista Vico, I was much taken with this idea, because it conformed to Vico's notion that the "logic" of all "poetic wisdom" was contained in the relationships that language itself provided in the four principal modes of figurative representation: metaphor, metonymy, synecdoche, and irony. My own hunch—which I find confirmed in Hegel's reflections on the nature of nonscientific discourse—is that in any field of study that, like history, has not yet become disciplined to the point of constructing a formal terminological system for describing its objects, in the way that physics and chemistry have, it is the types of figurative discourse that dictate the fundamental forms of the data to be studied. This means that the shape of the relationships that will appear to be inherent in the objects inhabiting the field will in reality have been imposed on the field by the investigator in the very act of identifying and describing the objects that he finds there. The implication is that historians *constitute* their subjects as possible objects of narrative representation by the very language they use to *describe* them. And if this is the case, it means that the different kinds of historical interpretations that we have of the same set of events, such as the French Revolution as interpreted by Michelet, Tocqueville, Taine, and others, are little more than projections of the linguistic protocols that these historians used to prefigure that set of events prior to writing their narratives of it. It is only a hypothesis, but it seems possible that the conviction of the historian that he has "found" the form of his narrative in the events themselves, rather than imposed it upon them, in the way the poet does, is a result of a certain lack of linguistic self-consciousness which obscures the extent to which descriptions of events already constitute interpretations of their nature. As thus envisaged, the difference between Michelet's and Tocqueville's accounts of the Revolution does not reside only in the fact that the former emplotted his story in the modality of a romance and the latter his in the modality of tragedy; it resides as well in the tropological mode—metaphorical and metonymic respectively—which each brought to his apprehension of the facts as they appeared in the documents.

I do not have the space to try to demonstrate the plausibility of this hypothesis, which is the informing principle of my book *Metahistory*. But I hope that this essay may serve to suggest an approach to the study of such discursive prose forms as historiography, an approach that is as old as the study of rhetoric and as new as modern linguistics. Such a study would proceed along the lines laid out by Roman Jakobson when he characterized the difference between Romantic poetry and the various forms of nineteenth-century realistic prose as residing in the essentially metaphorical nature of the former and the essentially metonymical nature of the latter.[6] I think that this characterization of the difference between poetry and prose is too narrow, because it presupposes that complex macrostructural narratives such as the novel are little more than projections of the "selective" (i.e., phonemic) axis of all speech acts. Poetry, and especially Romantic poetry, is then characterized by Jakobson as a projection of the "combinatory" (i.e., morphemic) axis of language. Such a binary theory pushes the analyst toward a dualistic opposition between poetry and prose, which appears to rule out the possibility of a metonymical poetry and a metaphorical

6. Roman Jakobson, "Linguistics and Poetics," in *Style in Language,* ed. Thomas A. Sebeok (Cambridge, Mass., and New York: M.I.T. Press and John Wiley, 1960), pp. 350–77.

prose. But the fruitfulness of Jakobson's theory lies in its suggestion that the various forms of both poetry and prose, all of which have their counterparts in narrative in general and therefore in historiography too, can be characterized in terms of the dominant trope which serves as the paradigm, provided by language itself, of all significant relationships conceived to exist in the world by anyone wishing to represent those relationships in language.

Narrative, or the syntagmatic dispersion of events across a temporal series presented as a prose discourse, in such a way as to display their progressive elaboration as a comprehensible form, would represent the "inward turn" that discourse takes when it tries to show the reader the true form of things existing behind a merely apparent formlessness. Narrative style, in history as well as in the novel, would then be construed as the modality of the movement from a representation of some original state of affairs to some subsequent state. The primary meaning of a narrative would then consist of the destructuration of a set of events (real or imagined) originally encoded in one tropological mode and the progressive restructuration of the set in another tropological mode. As thus envisaged, narrative would be a process of decodation and recodation in which an original perception is clarified by being cast in a figurative mode different from that in which it came encoded, by convention, authority, or custom. And the explanatory force of the narrative would then depend on the contrast between the original encodation and the later one.

For example, let us suppose that a set of experiences comes to us as a grotesque—i.e., as unclassified and unclassifiable. Our problem is to identify the modality of the relationships that bind together the discernible elements of the formless totality in such a way as to make of it a whole of some sort. If we stress the similarities among the elements, we are working in the mode of metaphor; if we stress the differences among them, we are working in the mode of metonymy. Of course, in order to make sense of any set of experiences, we must obviously identify both the parts of a thing that appear to make it up and the nature of the shared aspects of the parts that make them identifiable as a totality. This implies that all original characterizations of anything must utilize both metaphor and metonymy in order to "fix" it as something about which we can meaningfully discourse.

In the case of historiography, the attempts of commentators to make sense of the French Revolution is instructive. Burke recodes the events of the Revolution, which his contemporaries experience as a grotesque, in the mode of irony; Michelet recodes events in the mode of synecdoche; Tocqueville recodes them in the mode of metonymy. In each case, however, the movement from code to recode is narratively described, i.e., laid out on a time line in such a way as to make the interpretation of the events that make up the Revolution a kind of drama that we can recognize as satirical, romantic, and tragic respectively. This drama can be followed by the reader of the narrative in such a way as to be experienced as a progressive revelation of what the true nature of the events consists of. This revelation is not experienced, however, as a restructuring of perception so much as an illumination of a field of occurrence. But actually what has happened is that a set of events originally encoded in one way is simply being decoded by being recoded in another. The events themselves are not substantially changed from one account to another. That is to say, the data that are to be analyzed are not significantly different in the different accounts. What is different are the modalities of their relationships. These modalities, in turn, although they may appear to the reader to be based on different theories of the nature of society, politics, and history, ultimately have their origin in the figurative characterizations of the whole set of events as representing wholes of fundamentally different sorts. It is for this reason that, when it is a matter of setting different interpretations of the same set of historical phenomena over against one another in an attempt to decide which is the best or most convincing, we are often driven to confusion or ambiguity. This is not to say that we cannot distinguish between good and bad historiography, since we can always fall back on such criteria as responsibility to the rules of evidence, the relative fullness of narrative detail, logical consistency, and the like to determine this issue. But it is to say that the effort to distinguish between good and bad interpretations of a historical event such as the Revolution is not as easy as it might at first appear when it is a matter of dealing with alternative interpretations produced by historians of relatively equal learning and conceptual sophistication. After all, a great historical classic cannot be disconfirmed or nullified either by the discovery of some new datum that might call a specific explanation of some element of the whole account into question or by the generation of new methods of analysis that permit us to deal with questions that earlier historians might not have taken under consideration. And it is precisely because great historical classics, such as works by Gibbon, Michelet, Thucydides, Mommsen, Ranke, Burckhardt, Bancroft, and so on, cannot be definitively disconfirmed that we must look to the specifically literary aspects of their work as crucial, and not merely subsidiary, elements in their historiographical technique.

What all this points to is the need to revise the distinction conventionally drawn between poetic and prose discourse in discussion of such narrative forms as historiography and to recognize that the distinction, as old as Aristotle, between history and poetry obscures as much as it illuminates about both. If there is an element of the historical in all poetry, there is an element of poetry in every historical account. This is because in our account of the historical world we are dependent, in ways perhaps that we are not in the natural sciences, on the techniques of figurative language both for our characterization of the objects of our narrative representations and for the strategies by which to constitute narrative accounts of the transformations of those objects in time. And this is because history has no stipulatable subject matter uniquely its own; it is always written as part of a contest between contending poetic figurations of what the past *might* consist of.

The older distinction between fiction and history, in which fiction is conceived as the representation of the imaginable and history as the representation of the actual, must give place to the recognition that we can only know the actual by contrasting it with or likening it to the imaginable. As thus conceived, historical narratives are complex structures in which a world of experience is imagined to exist under at least two modes, one of which is encoded as "real," the other of which is "revealed" to have been illusory in the course of the narrative. Of course, it is a fiction of the historian that the various states of affairs that he constitutes as the beginning, the middle, and the end of a course of development are all "actual" or "real" and that he is merely recording "what happened" in the transition from the inaugural to the terminal phase. But both the beginning state of affairs and the ending one are inevitably poetic constructions, and as such are dependent upon the modality of the figurative language used to give them the appearance of coherence. This implies that all narrative is not simply a recording of "what happened" in the transition from one state of affairs to another, but is a progressive redescription of sets of events in such a way as to dismantle a structure encoded in one verbal mode in the beginning so as to justify a recoding of it in another mode at the end. This is what the "middle" of all narratives consists of.

All of this is highly schematic, and insistence on the fictive element in all historical narratives is certain to arouse the ire of historians who believe that they are doing something fundamentally different from the novelist by virtue of the fact that they deal with "real," while the novelist deals with "imagined," events. But neither the form nor the explanatory power of narrative derives from the different contents it is presumed to be able to accommodate. In point of fact, history—the real world as it evolves in time—is made sense of in the same way that the poet or novelist tries to make sense of it, i.e., by endowing what originally appears as problematical and mysterious with the aspect of a recognizable, because it is a familiar, form. It does not matter whether the world is conceived to be real or only imagined, the manner of making sense of it is the same.

So, too, to say that we make sense of the real world by imposing upon it the formal coherence that we customarily associate with the products of writers of fiction in no way detracts from the status as knowledge that we ascribe to historiography. It would only detract from it if we were to believe that literature did not teach us anything about reality, but was a product of an imagination that was not of this world but of some other, inhuman, one. In my view, we experience the "fictionalization" of history as an "explanation" for the same reason that we experience great fiction as an illumination of a world that we inhabit along with the author. In both we re-cognize the forms by which consciousness both constitutes and colonizes the world it seeks to inhabit comfortably.

Finally, it may be observed that if historians were to recognize the fictive element in their narratives, this would not mean the degradation of historiography to the status of ideology or propaganda. In fact, this recognition would serve as a potent antidote to the tendency of historians to become captive of ideological preconceptions, which they do not recognize as such but honor as the "correct" perception of "the way things really are." By drawing historiography nearer to its origins in literary sensibility, we should be able to identify the ideological, because it is the fictive, element in our own discourse. We are always able to see the "fictive" element in those historians with whose interpretations of a given set of events we disagree; we seldom perceive that element in our own prose. So, too, if we recognized the literary or fictive element in every historical account, we would be able to move the teaching of historiography onto a higher level of self-consciousness than it currently occupies.

What teacher has not lamented his inability to give instruction to apprentices in the writing of history? What graduate student of history has not despaired at trying to comprehend and imitate the model that his instructors appear to honor but the principles of which remain uncharted? If we recognize that there is a fictive element in all historical narrative, we will find in the theory of language and narrative itself the basis for a more subtle presentation of what historiography consists of than that which simply tells the student to go and "find out the facts" and write them up in such a way as to tell "what really happened."

In my view, history as a discipline is in bad shape today because it has lost sight of its origins in the literary imagination. In the interest of appearing scientific and objective, it has repressed and denied to itself its own greatest source of strength and renewal. By drawing historiography back once more to an intimate connection with its literary basis, we will be not only putting ourselves on guard against merely ideological distortions, we will be arriving at that "theory" of history without which it cannot pass for a "discipline" at all.

Kieran Egan

3
THUCYDIDES,
TRAGEDIAN

It is now about three-quarters of a century since the publication of
F. M. Cornford's *Thucydides Mythistoricus*.[1] In this work Cornford
argues that a proper reading of Thucydides' *History* shows that it was
profoundly influenced by "the tragic theory of human nature—a traditional psychology which Thucydides seems . . . to have learnt from
Aeschylus" (p. x). This tragic theory of human nature performs a
determining role in "the selection of incidents that should serve as a
record of the reality and the proportions and perspectives assigned to
them" (p. 129) and ensures that Thucydides, despite his stated intentions, "left the plane of pedestrian history for the 'more serious philosophic' plane of poetry" (p. 126). In so doing, he shapes all "that
misery and suffering into the thing of beauty and awe which we call
tragedy" (p. 250). Thus, what begins as "a textbook of strategy and
politics" (p. vii) becomes "a lesson in morality" (p. 127).

This argument implies that the nineteenth- and early-twentieth-cen-
tury scholars who adopted Thucydides as the precocious fountainhead
of "scientific" historiography were guilty of a seriously anachronistic
reading. Cornford claims that interpretation of events is "controlled"
in every age "by some scheme of unchallenged and unsuspected presuppositions" (p. viii), and that modern readers of Thucydides, finding
him trustworthy on matters of detail, ignore the residue of mythical
presuppositions and read him as a historian with aims and concerns
similar to their own. The prevailing opinion, which Cornford calls the
"Modernist Fallacy" (p. x), is exemplified in Bury's judgment at the
turn of the century: "The first History, in the true sense of the word,
sprang full-grown into life, like Athena from the brain of Zeus."[2]

Since the minor sensation of its first appearance, the argument of
Thucydides Mythistoricus has found little favor. Shortly after its pub-

1. *Thucydides Mythistoricus* (London: Edward Arnold, 1907). Subsequent references to this work will be made in the text.
2. J. B. Bury, *A History of Greece*, 3rd ed. (1900; rpt. London: Macmillan, 1963), p.
398.

lication, Bury himself acknowledged Cornford's "brilliant study," but concluded that "the occasional use of tragic irony cannot be held to have more than a stylistic significance."[3] And while serious students of Thucydides still acknowledge the stimulation of Cornford's reading, it is generally concluded that the emphasis he gives the note of tragedy in the *History of the Peloponnesian War* is, at best, disproportionate, and that concern with mythical influence in this most rational of authors is misplaced and irrelevant to a proper understanding of the work.

The question raised by Cornford concerns the proper epistemological status of Thucydides' *History;* either it should be classified as "scientific" historiography, or it is so profoundly infected with a particular myth-determined preconception that it should be classed as a tragedy that uses actual incidents in its composition. I will argue that Cornford was right; it is as sensible to call Thucydides the fourth Greek tragedian from whom a work has survived virtually entire as to call him a historian in what we recognize, more or less, with Bury as "the true sense of the word."

In Section I, therefore, I will try to show that Thucydides' stated purpose in writing the *History,* and the style in which he fulfills that purpose, support Cornford's reading; in Section II, I will recast Cornford's argument that the notion of causality operating in the work is, in an important sense, myth-determined; in Section III, I will indicate why the speeches might properly be seen as key elements in molding the account of Athens' fall into a tragic form; and in Section IV, I will draw on Aristotle to provide further reasons for reading the *History* as a tragedy. Finally I will discuss some implications of my conclusions for the current debate on causality and for the methodology of analyzing historical and other narratives.

I

It is no wonder that Thucydides' *History* has spawned an enormous critical literature. It is surely one of the most remarkable documents we have. Its concentration of style is almost unmatched; even though it is tortuous, many a writer would give an arm to be able to write a line with the austerity and authority that Thucydides brings to most of the book. Bury considers it "severe in its reserves, written from a purely intellectual point of view, unencumbered with platitudes and moral judgements, cold and critical."[4] Certainly, the style is severe

3. *The Ancient Greek Historians* (1909; rpt. New York: Dover, 1958), p. 124.
4. *History of Greece,* p. 399.

and cold. Collingwood asks "what is the matter with the man that he writes like that?"[5] It might be less wise to accept Collingwood's explanation—that Thucydides had a "bad conscience" for not writing proper history—than to recognize in his style that Yeatsian ideal, to write something "as cold and passionate as the dawn."[6]

What is the reason for this cold passion that drove Thucydides for more than thirty years to check and recheck endless details? Why this concentrated austerity with which he records minor skirmishes of little significance, the names of otherwise nameless commanders in tiny conflicts and of ship captains in inconsequential naval maneuvers? Herodotus is sure to give an interesting snippet or a good story in his asides, but Thucydides provides meticulously verified details with hardly a trace of explicit conjecture, leaving the dominant impression of "that strong, severe, hard factuality."[7] As Cornford noted, "Socrates appears, in comparison, superstitious" (*Th. Myth.*, p. 74).

Thucydides says that he wrote this way to prevent the Peloponnesian War from sliding over into myth like the Trojan War, which had been left to the poets to record. Did he do it all for a love of "factuality" then, to record *wie es eigentlich gewesen war,* in best scientific tradition? The reason he gives differs in a significant way from such a notion. He wrote his *History* to be useful to "those who want to understand clearly the events which happened in the past and which (human nature being what it is) will, at some time or other and in much the same ways, be repeated in the future."[8] To read this as unexceptionable proof of his pragmatism or of his acceptance of a Platonic cyclical view of history seems too facile. Despite various possible interpretations, however, it seems reasonable to assume that Thucydides was describing something other than, or in addition to, a desire to record facts for their own sake.

Commentators have recognized in the *History* the aim not just to record facts accurately but also to establish some more general truths.

5. R. G. Collingwood, *The Idea of History* (Oxford: Clarendon, 1946; rpt. New York: Oxford Univ. Press, 1956), p. 29.

6. W. B. Yeats, "The Fisherman," *The Collected Poems* (London: Macmillan, 1961), pp. 166–67.

7. Friedrich Nietzsche, *Twilight of the Idols,* rpt. in *The Portable Nietzsche,* trans. and ed. Walter Kaufmann (New York: Viking, 1954), p. 558.

8. Thucydides, *History of the Peloponnesian War,* trans. Rex Warner (Harmondsworth, Eng.: Penguin Books, 1954), I.22; p. 24. Except where stated, I use Warner's translation. Subsequent references to the *History* will be made in the text. I will give first the classical reference, followed by a page reference to the Warner 1954 translation, not the 1972 revision.

This craving for generality is usually described as typical of ancient Greek thinkers. Finley noted their ability to reduce actualities "to their generic and hence their lasting patterns"; or, as he put it later, Thucydides seems to have thought he would be able to "write a paradigm of wars between great states."[9]

Thucydides frequently repeats that he aims to give a true picture of events, and each time he suggests as a rider that this knowledge will be useful when these or similar events recur. After his account of the Corcyrean revolution, he draws the more general conclusion: "In the various cities these revolutions were the cause of many calamities—as happens and always will happen while human nature is what it is"; though here he adds that "the general rules will admit of some variety" (III.82; p. 208). He uses similar language after describing the typical progress of the plague in its victims; his stated purpose is to "set down the symptoms, knowledge of which will enable it to be recognized, if it should ever break out again" (II.48; pp. 123–24).

His attitude toward the plague is as appropriate as the language he uses to describe it. This section reads like the very best of the Hippocratic canon—a precise description of the characteristics of the disease, its progress to climax, and its typical conclusion—all without unnecessary "philosophizing." The similarity has often been noted between this treatment of the plague and his approach to, and language about, the Corcyrean revolution and the war in general. A number of commentators have pointed to the obvious parallels to illustrate Thucydides' "scientific" approach to historiography. How far, though, is a method appropriate to the study of sickness equally appropriate to the study of human affairs? The course of a disease and the events of human history would normally be distinguished on the grounds that one is limited and prescribable and the other is indeterminate. The claim that a detailed record of one historical event may serve as a paradigm for a whole series of other events classified under the same heading would normally be considered antihistorical.

The similarities between recording the symptoms of the plague and the events of the war for the use of posterity seem no more than a rough analogy, but it is not clear from anything in the text that Thucydides makes the distinction we tend to read into it. He seems rather to believe that by recording precisely what *happened,* he will also, because of the constants in "the nature of human things," expose some-

9. John H. Finley, Jr., *Thucydides* (Cambridge, Mass.: Harvard Univ. Press, 1942), p. 325, and *Four Stages of Greek Thought* (Stanford: Stanford Univ. Press, 1966), p. 57.

thing of what *happens* (to borrow Frye's useful way of making Aristotle's distinction[10]). That is, he is not interested in the particularities of events primarily for their own sake, but rather for the regularities or "general rules" or laws that may be revealed operating in them. It may be farfetched to see this as a conscious, out-and-out search for some Platonic paradigm, but his evident search for some more general truths or laws about human events—not dissimilar in kind from those obtainable from a precise study of the symptoms of a disease—cannot be sensibly denied.

If Thucydides aimed to describe both what *happened* between Athens and Sparta, and also what *happens* when strife arises between states, then the latter part of his aim represents what Aristotle refers to as the "philosophic" enterprise that should distinguish the poet's from the historian's work. Yet the proficiency with which Thucydides fulfills the former part of his aim tends to disarm most modern readers. Abbott goes so far as to laud Thucydides' foresight: "Thrice has modern Europe been rent by a conflict in essence similar to the Peloponnesian War."[11] Abbott's readiness to recognize "essential" similarities between the Peloponnesian War and modern European conflicts is compatible with Thucydides' purpose in leaving such a description that posterity might recognize similar events when they recur and, knowing the "general rules," be better able to deal with them. Thucydides surely did think that he had captured some "essence" of interstate conflicts, since he commends his work to us with such confidence as a possession forever. Yet the conclusion of this line of thinking is that we need write no more histories after the essential types of events have been meticulously described; we need only to classify new examples under the established paradigms. This aim of Thucydides', of course, and the perceptive intelligence he brings to it, accounts for his reputation as the father of scientific history. The Marxists particularly see him as the fountainhead of that tradition of historiography, leading to Marx himself, that aimed to derive empirically demonstrable inductive laws from the study of particular events.

Wherever we wish to stand on the methodological propriety or possibility of what Thucydides attempted, it is clear that he did not share modern historians' interest in events for their own sake or for the sake of low-level generalization. His primary reason for studying

10. Northrop Frye, "New Directions from Old," in *Fables of Identity: Studies in Poetic Mythology* (New York: Harcourt, Brace & World, 1963).

11. G. F. Abbott, *Thucydides: A Study in Historical Reality* (London: George Routledge, 1925), p. 3.

what happened was the desire and expectation of uncovering the laws that govern what happens in human affairs.

It is worth noting here that the tragedians also used particular incidents to body forth some more general truth about the nature of things. Aristotle argues that it is irrelevant to the tragedian's purpose whether the incidents he uses are historical; true incidents can be used quite as effectively as invented ones. What determines whether the author is a poet or historian is not the sort of incident he uses, but rather whether he employs incidents in order to relate some more universal truth about man in the world rather than merely the details of what happened. Plotting concerns the way incidents are causally related.

We will not want to accuse Thucydides of "mythologizing" because his concern seems superficially akin to the poet's aim of embodying with incidents the mythoi that reflect the universally true in human affairs. But if it can be shown that Thucydides' emplotment of incidents is determined by a particular mythos—that common to tragedies—then we may say that the laws he searched for were in fact held, no doubt unconsciously, as a priori truths. That is, he was not engaged in the scientific enterprise of deriving laws from his study of particulars, but rather he was involved in the poetic enterprise of selecting and molding particulars to body forth truths held a priori. Let us see how this may be supported by an examination of the sense of causality apparent in his *History*.

II

One of the main foundations Cornford develops for his argument arose from his analysis of Thucydides' notion of causality. He makes the case at considerable length that Thucydides, again despite his stated intention, never accounts satisfactorily for the causes of the war, and that the sense of causality that operates throughout the work is more appropriate to drama than to historiography. Cornford suggests that this is so because Thucydides lacks an adequate "apparatus of scientific conceptions" (*Th. Myth.*, p. ix), and so depends on a poetic or dramatic paradigm for his causal connections. In somewhat of an overstatement of his case, Cornford claims that, to the ancient Greeks, "Human affairs—the subject matter of history—were not a single strand in the illimitable web of natural evolution; their course was shaped solely by one or both of two factors: immediate human motives, and the will of gods and spirits, of Fortune or of Fate. The rationalist who rejected the second class was left with the first alone— the original and uncaused acts of human wills" (*Th. Myth.*, p. 68).

Cornford concludes that Thucydides does not try to answer what we understand by the question, "What were the causes of the war?" but, rather, something like the questions, "What were the beginning or first acts of the war, and what were the grievances of the groups that led up to them?" So the "first book is not an analysis of causes, but the story of a quarrel" (*Th. Myth.*, p. 59). Let us reconsider the plausibility of this conclusion.

To avoid any doubt about what led to this great war falling on the Hellenes, Thucydides describes three different kinds of causes: first, the grievances or reasons for disaffection between the parties; second, specific instances in which their different interests clashed; and third, he declares, in Sealey's precise translation, that the "truest cause, though least spoken of, was, in my opinion, that the Athenians, who were growing powerful and arousing alarm among the Lacedaemonians, compelled them to make war."[12]

It certainly seems that "Athens was spoiling for a fight."[13] In other contexts, significantly not given as systematic support for his claim that Athens compelled Sparta to fight, he tells of a series of aggressive Athenian moves. Her decision to aid Corcyra was certainly provocative, as were the exorbitant demands made on the Potidaeans, and Phormio's attack on the Amraciots, and, not least, the strict maintenance of the Megarian decrees. Athens' aggressive stance is, perhaps, best represented in the speech given by the Athenians who happened to be in Sparta at the first debate. Thucydides says that they asked to speak, "not that they had any intention of defending themselves" (I.72; p. 52), but because they simply wanted to show the Spartans "what sort of city [they would] have to fight against, if [they made] *the wrong decision*" (I.73; p. 52; my italics). They ended with a threat: if the Spartans responded to Athens' provocations by engaging in war, they would be met "in any and every field of action that [they] may choose" (I.78; p. 57). This, after gratuitous insults about the gaucheness of Spartans abroad.

Athenian aggression, as far as we can tell from Thucydides, seems to be prompted by fear that the Corcyrean fleet will be absorbed by the Peloponnesian forces in the war which the Athenians see as inevitable. Sparta is forced to act from fear of Athens' aggressive and expanding power. So the motives of action are ultimately psychological. Cities are personified early on and are given psychological characteristics: Athens is quick, daring, and inventive; Sparta is slothful

12. R. Sealey, "Thucydides, Herodotus and the Causes of War," *Classical Quarterly*, 7, No. 1 (1957), 9.

13. Ibid.

and dull. Sparta seems afraid of what will happen to her, and Athens seems afraid that her imperialist expansion will be inhibited. These ultimate causes of behavior might be satisfactory in a drama, in which characters usually act from fear or some other emotion, but they are surely inadequate in analyzing the causes of a war between states. Such an account is comprehensible as drama, but inadequate as a historical analysis of causes. There is a whole area that we consider essential for a proper understanding of the causes of a war that Thucydides ignores altogether, what Momigliano has called "the remote causes," in contrast to "immediate causes," which he thinks Thucydides does provide. "The remote causes of a war are as much plain facts as the immediate causes. If the facts are not produced, if we are left with a vague feeling of mystery, then we can be certain we have been misled."[14]

Where has Thucydides misled us, and why? Part of the answer—the "where"—lies in the opaqueness that persists despite his intention to ensure clarity about the causes of the war. In arguing that Cornford's "main thesis still contains a great deal of truth," Momigliano repeats his conclusion that "Thucydides tried to understand the mind of the people who decided to fight rather than the traditions and interests that were involved in the fight." This has ensured that we still argue about responsibility for the war with insufficient evidence, and, as Momigliano regretfully notes: "The whole of the diplomatic and social history of the thiry years before the Peloponnesian War is perhaps irretrievably lost for us just because Thucydides was not interested in it. There are so many things we do not know because Thucydides did not care to study them."[15] Cornford, and more recently Kitto and de Romilly,[16] have pointed up some of the areas that we would investigate if we were to give an account of the events Thucydides deals with, but which he passes over in silence.

The "where" may be further clarified by a close look at those areas in which Thucydides says something is in the nature of human things. To say that something is natural or inevitable is to put a "stopper" on further questions. That is, if we believe something is natural, we do not then ask why it is natural. Looking for subtle "stoppers" in Thucydides' *History*—elements he considers natural that we might

14. Arnaldo Momigliano, *Studies in Historiography* (London: Weidenfeld and Nicolson, 1966), p. 117.

15. Ibid., pp. 117, 118.

16. H. D. F. Kitto, *Poiesis* (Berkeley: Univ. of California Press, 1966), esp. pp. 259–79; Jacqueline de Romilly, *Thucydides and Athenian Imperialism,* trans. Philip Thody (Oxford: Blackwell, 1963), esp. Pt. 1.

want to inquire further into—will also help in answering the more interesting question, *Why* has Thucydides misled us?

Cornford's answer to the "why" part of the question is incomplete and confusing. His case seems to become buried under massive and suspect erudition, and the connections among primitive spirits, Aeschylus' stage, and Thucydides' *History* seem often spun out of little more than Cornford's own ingenuity. He concludes, nevertheless, that Thucydides fails to explain the causes of the war because "he never understood them" (*Th. Myth.*, p. x), and claims that "Thucydides has not told us the causes, and one reason for this omission is that he never raised the question, and never could raise it, in distinct and unambiguous terms" (*Th. Myth.*, p. 59). I think it is possible to sustain this conclusion by passing over Cornford's own detailed analysis of the spiritual predecessors of *apate, peitho, fortuna, elpis,* and so on, and, ironically, by drawing instead on the work of one of his severest critics.

C. N. Cochrane argues that Thucydides is a "scientific" historian who drew on and adapted the methodology of Hippocratic medicine, the most advanced empirical science of his day. Cochrane, and many others who have aimed to show how "scientific" or "realistic" Thucydides is, seem to have assumed that establishing this connection overthrew Cornford's argument that Thucydides' text is determined by mythical elements. It is generally recognized now that Thucydides does have significant methodological commonalities with Hippocrates, and that Cochrane exaggerates these and exaggerates their modernity as well. Establishing a reasonable claim for the "scientific" methodology that Thucydides may have adopted from Hippocrates, however, does not undermine Cornford's main conclusion but actually serves to clarify and strengthen it.

Cochrane argues that in "the fifth century B.C., at least in the one department of medicine, genuine science had emerged among the Greeks; and the power and originality of Thucydides lies in his having attempted to adopt the principles of that science to the study of society." He suggests, further, that "Thucydides supplied, so to speak, the counter-part in history" to the work of the "great Greek naturalists, from Thales to Democritus," who "had boldly faced the problem of the cosmos, and sought to wring from nature her secret."[17] Thucydides and Hippocrates surely do belong in that great tradition of Greek thinkers who sought to wring from nature her secret, and they set about it in a manner that is familiar and realistic, compared to that of

17. C. N. Cochrane, *Thucydides and the Science of History* (London: Oxford Univ. Press, 1929), pp. 15, 169.

most of their predecessors. The Hippocratic author of *Ancient Medicine* says his aim is to discover the physical nature of man and attain an accurate knowledge of causation in this field (Ch. XX). This sounds similar to Thucydides' stated aim in his chosen field of inquiry. Their methods have much in common too: they eschew working from "general hypotheses," and rely heavily on precise observation and meticulous description; they share a remarkable detachment from what they describe so carefully, and a lofty rejection of divine causes for inexplicable changes in the phenomena they observe; they share also what Jones (describing Hippocrates) has called a "clear, dignified—even majestic"[18] style and attitude.

Yet, extending Cornford's advice, a study of Hippocrates should begin, not like Cochrane's, by examining his most "modern" features, but rather by studying "his *a priori* forms of thought."[19] We should look, in Cornford's words, at his "scheme of unchallenged and unsuspected presuppositions," that "circumambient atmosphere of his place and time," and see whether we might not sensibly consider Hippocrates' work as significantly influenced by myth.

Whatever may remain debatable about Kuhn's theory of scientific revolutions,[20] he has shown clearly how each paradigm-generation tends to rewrite and falsely reinterpret the conclusions of its predecessors as though their concerns, methods, and viewpoints were similar. This procedure is evident in Cochrane's book to the extent that Hippocrates is presented as an incipient behaviorist with a modern outlook. If one were to read Cochrane before Hippocrates, the latter would come as rather a surprise. One would certainly be unprepared for his basic concerns. It would be difficult to make much sense of the Hippocratic corpus, for instance, without knowledge of the theory of humors and the derivation of that theory. Cochrane is silent here, as though the theory of humors were as irrelevant to Hippocrates' ideas about medicine as it is to ours.

Cochrane writes of the great tradition of Greek naturalists who sought to wring from nature her secret. Thales, at the fountainhead of this tradition, declared that everything was made of water. Such a

18. W. H. S. Jones, Introduction to *Hippocrates,* trans. W. H. S. Jones (London: Heinemann, 1923), p. xv.

19. Later, when responding to attacks on some parts of his argument, Cornford reasserted his belief "that the criticism of an ancient historian should begin with the study of his *a priori* forms of thought" (*Proceedings of the Classical Association,* 1921; rpt. in Cornford, *The Unwritten Philosophy and Other Essays,* ed. W. K. C. Guthrie [Cambridge: Cambridge Univ. Press, 1967]).

20. Thomas S. Kuhn, *The Structure of Scientific Revolutions,* International Encyclopedia of Unified Science, Vol. 2, No. 2 (Chicago, Chicago Univ. Press, 1962).

hypothesis is extremely odd if Thales "boldly faced the problem of the cosmos" without some set of presuppositions, some context of a priori beliefs, that make his conclusion sensible. What kinds of presuppositions would lead someone to conclude that everything was made of water? Indeed, why should anyone conclude that everything was made from some ultimate material in the first place? To make sense of Thales, we need to understand the circumambient atmosphere of *his* place and time just as we do for Hippocrates and Thucydides. A study of that atmosphere or, better, the person's a priori forms of thought, will clarify what elements of his thinking were determined, and allow us to appreciate more fully what elements were "free" or original. This procedure is followed not to diminish earlier thinkers but simply as necessary to understand them properly.

But, of course, the cosmos does not present us with problems. To think that it does is to risk being misled by a useful metaphor. We pose to ourselves problems about the cosmos because of, and in response to, our peculiar requirements for making sense of things. Why do we share with Thales the question of what the world is made of and yet respond so differently? We inherit a range of inquiry from him, but we also inherit knowledge and expectations from his successors that determine our way of perceiving the world and the kinds of questions that it seems appropriate to ask. What kinds of questions, then, were the Milesian hylozoists responding to when they declared that the cosmos was made from some ultimate material and that the tangible world was composed of mixtures of earth, air, fire, and water? Prerational Greek speculation about the world described, in myths, increasingly depersonalized gods who ruled/represented elements of earth, air, fire, and water. When the Milesians swept away these gods, they preserved the divisions found as early as Homer's retelling of the cosmogonic myth, in which the world was divided into lots (*moirai*) between Zeus, Hades, and Neptune, while the earth was common to all (*Iliad,* XV. 187 ff.).[21] The free element of their thinking swept away gods and exposed the whole cosmos to rational inquiry and speculation. The determined part preserved the mythic paradigm according to which they inquired after an ultimate material from which the world was made, and the four elements in which things were divided. This determining paradigm obviously has a mythic source, and it is thus quite proper to say that the Milesians' inquiry was profoundly influenced by a mythic element.

21. In another flawed but enormously suggestive book, *From Religion to Philosophy* (London: Edward Arnold, 1912), Cornford succeeds in tracing the derivation of some seminal Greek ideas from Homer to the atomists.

It is not necessary to detail here the derivation of the doctrine of humors to see that it too has an obvious mythic ancestry, related closely to that of the theory of four elements, and that it determined thought about sickness quite rigidly. That is, the question it became appropriate to ask, the kinds of thing it became appropriate to observe, the way illness was perceived, were to some very significant degree determined by a paradigm derived from myth. As the beliefs necessary to sustain myth faded, that which accounted for certain features of the world in a myth story became a structural principle determining rational inquiries—from myth to mythos, as it were.

The sophistication of the best work in the Hippocratic canon may be measured by the degree to which precise observation leads the author to free himself from the cruder form of the paradigm. The idea that treatment should be by opposites—for a hot disease, cold should be prescribed, and for moist diseases, dry—is rejected as too simplistic, because observation shows that the body sometimes reacts to excess of cold by creating its own heat, as we may see from the burning and tingling of our feet at night after walking through snow (*Ancient Medicine,* Ch. XVI). But even here there is only a slight shift within the inherited paradigm. Good health is still considered a balance of opposites, particularly—and in the cruder works, exclusively—between the hot and the cold, the moist and the dry, or among the bodily fluids, the biles and phlegm and blood. Sickness is considered a matter of one element getting out of balance and, to use tendentious language, exceeding its proper bounds. A cure is to be sought by encouraging or causing the reinstitution of harmony. So, while observation may suggest more sophisticated ways of using the paradigm to interpret perception, it is clear that the paradigm plays, in all the Hippocratic texts, an important role in determining the way its users make sense of their observations.

A detailed analysis of the Hippocratic canon and an examination of the derivation of key presuppositions found in it, would, I think, sustain the general conclusions above. This is not to condemn the Hippocratics, but, rather, to suggest that their precise observations and original conclusions still carried a substantial burden from the proto-speculation of myth. It is in precisely this sense that Cornford tags Thucydides "Mythistoricus." Borrowing, then, some of Cochrane's conclusions about elements that Thucydides shared with Hippocrates, let us see whether they do not enlighten an important feature of Thucydides' *History* and support Cornford's general argument.

One of the closest connections established by Cochrane between

Hippocrates and Thucydides concerns the interpretation of causes. Sickness results from imbalance in the humors. The primary cause of such imbalance is "shock." Shock leads to stasis in the system. Hippocrates says that "shocks, striking the mind with great frequency, incite wildness, obscuring the qualities of mildness and gentleness."[22] Cochrane shows how Thucydides adapts his paradigm. The description of the plague follows closely the best work of the Hippocratic canon. But further, as Cochrane argues, the "canons of interpretation employed for the prognosis of the plague seem to us to be the canons employed also in the interpretation of Greek history generally."[23]

Certainly, the stasis at Corcyra follows the same pattern as in the plague. Disturbance of harmony follows on shocks that throw the social opposites of rich and poor into conflict. The symptoms of the stasis are described in meticulous detail up to the point of crisis. The results are noted in the eventual destruction of that which each side sought to dominate. Similarly, on a larger scale, the opposites of Athens and Sparta, the sea power and the land power, are shown in conflict (despite the prominence of other cities, like Corinth, and other interests, like those of the Persian Empire), their harmony having been destroyed by Athens' immoderate growth. The symptoms of their stasis are described in meticulous detail, and the resulting destruction of that harmony we call Hellenism, which each had sought to dominate, is carefully recorded.

If Thucydides' account of the war is similar in these ways to the Hippocratic method of accounting for sickness, the opaque features in his outline of the causes of the war are more readily understood, and it becomes possible to explain why he offers no account of "the remote causes" of the war and why he considers things "natural" that we think it proper to inquire about further.

Let us return to Thucydides' "truest cause," Athens' imperialism. After recounting the grievances between the parties, he digresses to develop the rise of Athenian power in some detail from the end of the Persian War to the beginning of the Peloponnesian War. Yet, here too, in the Pentecontaetia (I.89–117; pp. 62–76), he describes a further series of events that caused grievances that might have been resolved by arbitration or some kind of accommodation but led to war. This is Thucydides' analysis of the "truest cause." He felt no need to look at anything except the growth of Athenian power because this was the source of disharmony and was therefore a sufficient reason in the nature of things for the outbreak of war. Having

22. Cochrane, *Thucydides and the Science of History*, p. 109.
23. Ibid., p. 28.

isolated the "truest cause," he had only to describe the outbreak of symptoms, their course of development to crisis, and the result. This is why there is no analysis of remote causes. Because the growth of Athenian power led to imbalance within Greece, the outbreak of war was *natural*. Thucydides concludes his description of Athens' growth: "So finally the point was reached when Athens' strength attained a peak plain for all to see and the Athenians began to encroach upon Sparta's allies. It was at this point that Sparta felt the position to be no longer tolerable and decided by starting this present war to employ all her energies in attacking and, if possible, destroying the power of Athens" (I.118; p. 77).

The cause is presented as a matter of imbalance, something we still readily understand as a common metaphor for psychological impulses. The parties, the interests, and so on, that we would inquire into are ignored, because the paradigm—the circumambient atmosphere, the a priori forms of thought—that Thucydides shares with the Hippocratics has a built-in "stopper" on such inquiry. Strife is caused by imbalance. Therefore, if there is imbalance, strife will follow in the nature of things.

The historian's task is not to inquire why the nature of things is as it is, but simply to note this truth about human affairs, identify the source of the imbalance, describe the events immediately leading up to the outbreak, and then note as precisely as possible the course of the strife and its outcome. This is v   Thucydides does with matchless objectivity. I would go so far as to agree with Cornford, against Momigliano, that Thucydides does not even provide "immediate causes" for the war, except perhaps incidentally. I think it more proper to see these as "grievances," to use Cornford's word, or initial symptoms. Thucydides does not explain what interests determined, particularly in Athens, that the imperialist policy should erupt into a general war embroiling virtually every power in contact with the Greeks. Thinking that strife follows naturally on imbalance, there is no reason to focus on what we would consider the most significant contingencies—those, for example, that determine that a negotiable position should result in war.

There are, then, two kinds of causes giving movement to Thucydides' *History,* the one psychological and the other proceeding from necessity. That is, events are explained by reference to states of mind—"the fear of the Lacadaemonians," or by reference to what is natural in human affairs.

Thucydides, however, shares his notions of causality not only with the Hippocratics, but, much more fully, with the tragedians; what he considers natural in fact asserts a sense of causality that is central to the tragic world view. In the next section, I will consider how the speeches are used to give movement to the *History* both by expressing the psychological motives for events and by articulating the sense of necessity that Thucydides seems to have accepted a priori.

III

Thucydides says he will provide two elements: the speeches of the main parties in the conflict and the deeds that followed from them. Cornford argues that this is precisely what he does, and that he provides no causes as a modern historian would understand them. The speeches take up nearly one quarter of the text and show the feelings of the different groups. Thucydides then shows what acts follow from these. The psychological causes of, or motives for, events are sought in the sentiments of the actors in the drama, whether individuals or personified cities, much as is the case on the stage. There is not space here for a detailed analysis of the relationships between the *logoi* and *erga* that make up Thucydides' *History*, but it is necessary to establish the manner in which the speeches are used in the structure of the work. If they are only a trivial anomaly, they will not seriously undermine our acceptance of Thucydides as the first historian "in the true sense of the word." They amount, however, to rather more than that.

Jaeger makes an apt comparison: "To do as some have done, and search these speeches for the relic of what was actually said on the occasion, is a task as hopeless as to try to recognize the features of the particular models in the gods sculpted by Phidias."[24] Clearly, the relationship of Thucydides' speeches to what was actually said on particular occasions varies considerably. In some cases he is, perhaps, quite close to the actual speech, and in others, the speech he gives is more or less of his own construction. Even though this varying relationship exists, he might nevertheless be expected to use speeches according to a consistent principle. He says that while trying to report accurately what was said, his "method has been . . . to make the speakers say what, in [his] opinion, was called for by each situation" (I.22; p. 24). If the criterion is literal accuracy, then Thucydides is criminally erratic. If, however, the criterion is based on the aim noted in the previous section of this essay, to uncover and show operating some more general truth about how things *happen,* then we may account for all the speeches as constructed according to a consistent principle, consistently applied.

24. Werner Jaeger, *Paideia,* trans. Gilbert Highet (New York: Oxford Univ. Press, 1939), 1:392.

The aim here is to suggest that Thucydides' use of speeches is closely akin to that of the dramatists—the speeches comment on the action, allot significance to events, echo with irony and prophecy, alert our expectations, and point up the moral and meaning of the work. Although the dramatic use of his speeches has been frequently pointed out, I want to argue that the manner of their use ensures more than a superficial similarity with drama, and their relationship with the events they accompany provides Thucydides with the means of organizing the history into the form of tragedy. Let us see what support can be given to such a reading by considering perhaps the most famous and vivid set of speeches, the Melian dialogue.

Here the narrative becomes entirely like that of a drama script. The scene is set. The inhabitants of Melos are colonists from Sparta who, unlike the other islanders, have courageously refused to submit to Athens. The Athenians have tried to coerce their submission by ravaging their lands, in response to which the Melians have taken up arms. Before leading their superior forces to almost certain victory, the Athenian generals send their envoys to negotiate. The overwhelming power of Athens impels the Melians to observe that the Athenians have come to judge, not to argue. If the Melian case is proven just, then war and their destruction must ensue, and if otherwise, their alternative is slavery. Thus the speeches begin, prefixed only by the names "Athenians," "Melians" in turn.

One curious fact about this event, to which Thucydides allots much space and implied significance, is that it is really very trivial in terms of the conduct of the war. The allegiance or otherwise of the Melians is of little strategic importance, and even their cruel fate is not remarkable in the run of this bloody war. We may, however, read it as one of his paradigms.

The main theme of the Athenian argument is that the Melians stand no chance of victory and should accept the dictates of superior force. They openly admit the innocence of the Melians: " . . . you, though a colony of Sparta, have not joined Sparta in the war . . . you have never done us any harm" (V.89; p. 360). Then Thucydides puts some remarkable statements into the mouths of the Athenians. "Our opinion of the gods and our knowledge of men lead us to conclude that it is a general and necessary law of nature to rule wherever one can. This is not a law that we made ourselves, nor were we the first to act upon it when it was made. We found it already in existence, and we shall leave it to exist for ever among those who come after us. We are merely acting in accordance with it . . . " (V.105; p. 363).

The Athenians tell the Melians that where matters of power are concerned the people of Greece think that there is no difference between right and wrong (V.97; p. 361). The Melians argue that they may still hope for some remarkable fortune in battle. The Athenians reply: "Hope, that comforter in danger! . . . hope is by nature an expensive commodity, and those who are risking their all on one cast find out what it means only when they are ruined" (V.103; p. 362). The Melians are further advised not to be led astray by some foolish notion of honor, because that is to be led by a mere idea to fall "voluntarily into irrevocable disaster, in dishonour that is all the more dishonourable because it has come to them from their own folly rather than their misfortune" (V.111; p. 364).

After hearing the Melian refusal to become their slaves, the Athenians depart with the words: "Well, at any rate, judging from this decision of yours, you seem to us quite unique in your ability to consider the future as something more certain than what is before your eyes, and to see uncertainties as realities, simply because you would like them to be so" (V.113; p. 365).

Their aim all along, they say, has simply been to get the Melians to "look the facts in the face" (V.87; p. 359). The result: "the Athenians . . . put to death all the men of military age whom they took, and sold the women and children as slaves" (V.116; p. 366).

Echoing Collingwood, one might note that there is still no good reason to revise Grote's judgment on the dialogue: "What we here read in Thucydides is in far larger proportion his own and in smaller proportion authentic report, than any of the other speeches which he professes to set down." Grote also comments on the dialogue's "surprising length, considering his general brevity."[25]

The dialogue comes with startling dramatic force after the subdued account of the indecisive battles and treaties of Book V, and it heralds the beginning of the Sicilian expedition. From the conclusion of the dialogue, the sentiments Thucydides thought proper to the situation, he turns immediately to this: "In the same winter the Athenians resolved to sail against Sicily with larger forces than those which Laches and Eurymedon had commanded, and, if possible, to conquer it. They were for the most part ignorant of the size of the island and the numbers of its inhabitants, both Hellenic and native, and they did not realize that they were taking on a war of almost the same magnitude as their war against the Peloponnesians" (VI.1; p. 367).

One motive that drove the Athenians to accept the Egestaean appeal that the Athenians should involve themselves further in Sicilian

25. George Grote, *History of Greece* (London: John Murray, 1862), 5:95.

affairs seems to have been a fear that the Dorian Syracusans would eventually help the Peloponnesians. But a stronger motive seems to have been the Egestaeans' promise of money, as well as their own extravagant ambition. After checking to see whether the money existed in the amounts promised, and having been deceived into believing it did, the Athenians vote for an expedition to be headed by Nicias and Alcibiades. In the hope of making the Athenians change their mind, Nicias asks them to reconsider whether it "is really a good thing . . . to send the ships at all?" He thinks they "ought not to give such hasty consideration to so important a matter and on the credit of foreigners get drawn into a war which does not concern [them]" (VI.9; p. 372). He is aware, he says, that no speech is likely to change the Athenians' character, and he will "therefore confine [himself] to showing [them] that this is the wrong time for such adventures and that the objects of [their] ambition are not to be gained easily" (VI.9; p. 372). Then his appeal becomes almost pathetic; he tells them to beware of Alcibiades, that "young man in a hurry" (VI.12; p. 375), who will risk the good of all for his own ambition. He begs them not to "indulge in hopeless passions for what is not there" (VI.13; p. 375).

But all to no avail. He cannot change their character—the ultimate "cause" of the expedition—which is reflected or embodied in Alcibiades. It is Alcibiades' will that prevails. He is introduced shortly before the Melian dialogue, his personal ambition dictating the policy he pursues with frenzied energy. Thucydides makes it clear that Alcibiades' passion to obtain the vote for the expedition to Sicily results from his personal ambition as a prospective commander and from the hope for glory and money which would allow him to support his extravagant life-style. Already he is demonstrating that crazy imbalance, that "quality in him which was beyond the normal" (VI.15; p. 376).

Significantly, he begins his speech by boasting that his extravagant show at the Olympics has persuaded the Hellenes to consider Athens "even greater than it really is" (VI.16; p. 376). Delusion is increasing. An argument he presents for the ease with which Sicily could be conquered is that there, "what each man spends his time on is trying to get from the public whatever he thinks he can get either by clever speeches or by open sedition—always with the intention of going off to live in another country, if things go badly with him" (VI.17; p. 378). This of course is precisely true of Alcibiades himself, and makes no sense applied to the Sicilians as a whole. He concludes his strategic arguments by assuring the Athenians that their security was guaranteed by their navy, "so that we can either stay there, if things go well, or come back again" (VI.18; p. 379). Irony and prophecy ring through the speeches.

After the failure of an earlier, small expedition to conquer Sicily, Thucydides says explicitly that the good sense of Pericles is being superseded; the Athenian judgment is infected with increasing wildness. "Such was the effect on the Athenians of their present good fortune that they thought nothing could go wrong with them; that the possible and the difficult were alike attainable, whether the forces employed were large or wholly inadequate. It was their surprising success in most directions which caused this state of mind and suggested to them that their strength was equal with their hopes" (IV.65; p. 266).

The Melian dialogue, preceding the Sicilian expedition and the reasons given for engaging in it, comes at a key turning point of the work. Although it is of little significance to the war, the dialogue is one of the most vivid and dramatic incidents of the work. This alone should alert us to the presence here of something more than a straightforward narration of events. Why is this incident given with such power immediately before the Sicilian expedition, with all these echoes and ironies and prophecies? Why is Athens to be recognized as morally blinded, before she is led by false hope and wild ambition to fight in Sicily? With a number of commentators, I can only conclude that Thucydides has organized this for dramatic purposes, although such a reading tends to be countered by arguments like Usher's: "In no case is it possible to demonstrate that fact or chronology have been distorted in order to give point to an antithesis. The artistry of Thucydides is the more remarkable for the fact that he does no more than underline the operation of forces inherent in the events themselves, without dramatic over-emphasis and without falsification"[26] The invention, however, of an entire dialogue that almost certainly never took place in anything like this form must be considered some kind of falsification, and if the echoes and ironies and prophecies in the Melian dialogue and the speeches preceding the Sicilian expedition are not dramatic overemphasis, then dramatic overemphasis is impossible. That there was a cold-blooded massacre of Melians is no doubt true. What is false is the dialogue with its pointed moral, and the prominence given to it.

Gomme rejects such a reading by asking: "Was Thucydides to put his events in the wrong order, or play down one of these two events,

---

26. Stephen Usher, *The Historians of Greece and Rome* (London: Hamish Hamilton, 1969), p. 65.

or insert some irrelevant twiddly bits . . . in order to avoid a dramatic contrast that was there in the events themselves?''[27] First, an insignificant event in the general campaign of keeping allies in line is hardly of equivalent importance in the war with the Sicilian expedition. The obvious point is not that he should play down either one, but that he has played up one out of any sensible proportion if his aim is to give a proportionate account of ''the events themselves.''

Why does this trivial side action contain the most intricate and dramatic speeches in the work? Why does the language echo with such terrible irony, the Athenians offering to the Melians precisely that advice they themselves fail to take, to their fatal cost, in the very next section of the work? It is grotesque to accept the drama as an accurate reflection of the events themselves, as though somehow in the reality there was a direct connection between a nonexistent debate on Melos and the launching of the Sicilian expedition.

One must also consider what it means to say that the drama resides in the events themselves. *No* meaning resides in the events themselves. Indeed, until the historian decides on his area of inquiry and begins to create discrete units from the changing process in time, ''events'' themselves do not exist. Reality is an ineffable process. ''Events'' are mental constructs, more or less crude tools that we create in order to make some sense of that process (and at best we seem unable to tell whether we are making sense of the process or making sense of the way we make sense of things).

Drama is an element of meaning, composed by creating and relating discrete events crudely hacked out of the process represented. To think that drama can reside in events themselves is simply a more sophisticated form of the pathetic fallacy. Drama cannot reside in events; it is derived from the manner of composing and organizing events.

Though the historian does not invent the process he tries to represent, he decides what units he will deal with and how they are to be related, and he can juxtapose certain kinds of events for dramatic purposes. This is what Thucydides does time and time again. Similarly, the sense of tragedy does not reside in the things done between Sparta and Athens, but is derived from Thucydides' skilled craftsmanship in creating proportion and significance and directing our perceptions and expectations of what is to follow.

Thucydides puts into the mouths of the speakers the sentiments he

27. A. W. Gomme, *The Greek Attitude to Poetry and History* (Berkeley: Univ. of California Press, 1954), p. 123.

thinks proper to their situation. What he sees is an Athens that has become increasingly unstable after the loss of Pericles' balanced guidance, the shocks resulting from the forcing of Attic country dwellers into the city, the plague, and the unforeseen successes and disasters of the war. Her wild ambition has led to false confidence and, as a result of blind folly, eventual disaster. Throughout the speeches warnings echo and reecho: it is in the nature of human things for those who put confidence in the future because of unexpected good fortune, resulting in false hope, pride, or ambition, to suffer eventual destruction. This theme is echoed at each key turning, and Athens ignobly rejects or foolishly ignores the warning again and again. It must be accentuated, however, that this method of using speeches to point up some universal moral, to underline some necessary movement of events, is the job of the dramatist, not the historian.

Just as the truest cause of the war is given as Sparta's fear of Athens' growth, so the truest cause of Athens' destruction is pointed up in the Melian dialogue. That is the purpose of the dialogue. The connection between an account of a nonexistent debate on Melos and the catastrophe in Sicily is that the former exposes the state of mind that causes the latter. The psychological state is called hybris, and it is the ultimate cause of the defeat to come. The "immediate causes," the initial symptoms, of the events that culminate in the harbor at Syracuse are described by Thucydides with his usual precision.

The general paradigm operating at the most profound level of the work is akin to that in Hippocrates. The proper condition of life involves a harmonious balance between the opposite elements of the system; if one element overlaps its proper bounds by reason of some chance or shock it causes stasis. If harmony is not reestablished, greater wildness infects the system, until the preternatural element or the system is destroyed. When this basic paradigm is adapted to human affairs, when morals and values are allotted to the elements, we have the prerequisites for a tragic world view. It is, then, a tragic paradigm—or mythos, or plot—that underlies Thucydides' *History* and asserts a tragic sense of causality. That is, the sense of tragedy is not derived from "the events themselves" but is present because Thucydides selected, ordered, valued, and interpreted events to body forth a sense of tragedy.

IV

So far it has been argued that Thucydides' *History* might best be understood as a combination of precise and original description articulated upon a paradigm derived from myth, a paradigm whose influence determines features of other kinds of inquiry, speculation, and modes of expression. The particular effect of this mythic paradigm, when it comes to representing social, political, and military processes, is to determine a view of them wherein a particular idea of necessity operates. This determines, in turn, the nature of causality perceived and so embodied in the *History*. And this sense of necessity is best known from its role in contributing to the effect proper to a tragedy.

The process whereby the events are articulated on the mythic paradigm may be described as "infiguration," to use Cornford's term. He makes a useful distinction between the processes he calls "infiguration" and "invention" with regard to fitting an account of events to some inherited pattern of thought or mythic paradigm:

> This process of *infiguration* . . . may be carried to any degree. Sometimes the facts happen to fit the mould, and require hardly any modification; mere unconscious selection is enough. In other cases they have to be stretched a little here, and patted down there, and given a twist before they will fit. In extreme instances, where a piece is missing, it is supplied by mythological inference from the interrupted portions which call for completion; and here we reach the other phase of the process, namely *invention*. This is no longer a matter of imparting a form to raw material; it is the creation of fresh material when the supply of facts is not sufficient to fill the mould. (*Th. Myth.*, p. 132)

When Thucydides regrets that his work will not be especially interesting because it lacks mythology, he seems to be referring to what Cornford calls "invention." When Cornford describes Thucydides as "Mythistoricus," he is referring primarily to his "infiguration"—the process whereby events are selected, composed, and connected in accordance with some determining "mould."

It is fairly easy to point up a number of superficial parallels between Thucydides' *History* and Aeschylean and, even more, Euripidean tragedy.[28] These superficial commonalities, however, are relatively insignificant in establishing the claim that Thucydides' *History* might sensibly be read as a tragedy. The commonality that needs to be established is at the level of plot—the very soul of tragedy.

Ultimately it is empirical evidence that determines whether a particular set of events constitutes a tragedy; the mechanism that tests any candidate is the gut, or sensibility. Thucydides' *History*, in my

28. See Cornford, *Thucydides Mythistoricus*, Ch. 8; and John H. Finley, Jr., *Three Essays on Thucydides* (Cambridge, Mass.: Harvard Univ. Press, 1967), esp. pp. 279–321.

experience, evokes the feeling that Aristotle describes as proper to tragedy. I will argue now, drawing heavily on Aristotle, that this is an appropriate response to the *History,* and that it is evoked by that soul of tragedy, the emplotment of the incidents.

In his rejection of Cornford's case, Finley points out that what interests Thucydides is the play of "larger social forces" and not the dealings and intentions of a group of "inscrutable gods."[29] But Thucydides' lack of gods is no objection to considering him a tragedian. The crucial element is a sense of inexorable and moral necessity, and all sensitive readers of Thucydides perceive this. Aristotle states that in the best tragedies "the unravelling of the plot . . . must arise out of the plot itself, it must not be brought about by the *deus ex machina.*"[30] Thucydides follows the proper course for the best tragic effect, allowing the events to body forth the unwinding necessity. Finley's own reading seems perceptive and true: "For all his rational optimism, Thucydides leaves no stronger impression than of the iron consequences of even a single error. Matchless as is his perception of issues, his gripping power lies also in the sheer urgency with which events unroll. This sense of ineluctability is in obvious conflict with his belief in reasoned choice. Though he gazed less fixedly than Euripides on this dark truth, its chilling presence as strongly moulds his work. Much of both men's power lies in their pursuing reason to the vision of its opposite."[31]

We might draw on Aristotle's authority to overcome what seem trivial but basic objections—that one cannot write a tragedy while representing real events in narrative form. Aristotle argues that "the poet or maker should be the maker of plots rather than of verses, since he is a poet because he imitates, and what he imitates are actions. And even if he chances to take an historical subject, he is none the less a poet" (IX.9).

So a tragedian is recognized not on the basis of his subject matter, but by the way he emplots the incidents he "imitates." Prior to this, Aristotle argues that if Herodotus had written in verse, he would still have been a historian, because the true difference between the poet and historian "is that one relates what has happened, the other what may happen. Poetry, therefore, is a more philosophical and higher thing than history: for poetry tends to express the universal, history the particular" (IX.3). I have argued that Thucydides does both: he

29. Finley, *Thucydides,* p. 324.

30. Aristotle, *Poetics,* trans. S. H. Butcher, 4th ed. (1932; rpt. New York: Hill and Wang, 1961), XV.7. Subsequent references to the *Poetics* will be made in the text.

31. Finley, *Four Stages,* p. 79.

relates what happened and attempts to show thereby what may happen in some more "universal" or "philosophical" sense.

Later Aristotle suggests that a tragedy "will differ in structure from historical compositions, which of necessity present, not a single action, but a single period, and all that happened within that period to one person or to many, little connected together as the events may be" (XXIII.1). Whomever Aristotle had in mind when writing this, we may be sure it was not Thucydides. When Aristotle writes about history and historians in the *Poetics*, he seems to have in mind perhaps Herodotus at his more disjointed moments, or some purer kind of annalist or chronologer. Thucydides ruthlessly concentrates on a "single action," whose beginning he recounts, whose middle or complication he follows in detail, and whose denouement he presents with terrible force.

The complexity and size of the *History* are not adequate objections to reading it as a tragedy. As Aristotle notes: "The greater the length, the more beautiful will the piece be by reason of its size, provided that the whole be perspicuous" (VII.7). Whatever elements Thucydides composed or revised very late in his life, he had undeniably succeeded in welding the two main periods of fighting and the many disparate events "to center round an action that in our sense of the word is one" (VIII.3).

The characteristic form and effect of Greek tragedy are built into the narrative by articulating the account of Athens' pride, blindness, and suffering onto the movement of the tragic emotion. (And it is worth noting that, while Thucydides is concerned with causes and events primarily in terms of psychological motivation, he is concerned with effects of events primarily in terms of human suffering.[32]) The *History* adheres to Aristotle's prescriptions for the best kind of tragedy: it is "complex" in Aristotle's sense: it excites pity and fear; it represents the downfall of a flawed character who was highly renowned and prosperous—Athens and her proud population—and who has "done or suffered something terrible"; its plot, "the structure of the incidents," is single in its issue; and it shows a reversal of fortune from good to bad. In addition, the characters in Thucydides' *History* are much more the types of tragedy than they are particular individuals. The proper role of character in tragedy, Aristotle says, is to reveal "moral purpose, showing what kinds of things a man chooses and avoids" (VI.17). The poet aims to express the "universal," that is, "how a person of a certain type will on occasion speak or act"

32. Kitto, *Poiesis*, Ch. 6, esp. pp. 270–79, 354.

(IX.4). Thucydides' characters are not unique individuals, but appear, rather, as "poetic" types, or almost as symbols: Pericles, the balanced man, preserver of harmony through modesty and foresight; Cleon, disproportionately violent and deluded; Alcibiades, bewitching and crazily ambitious; pious but inadequate Nicias. These elements constitute almost their entire personalities as Thucydides portrays them.

The moral that echoes through the speeches and is embodied in the events is that one should know oneself and keep within one's bounds. Blind ambition and improvident hope drive men to foolish actions, and the inevitable result is the loss even of what they had in the beginning. In a few persuasive paragraphs early in the work, Thucydides presents an ideal Athens that we cannot but love. Pericles warns her not to expand her empire during the war. Doom-laden language directs us to observe Athens' mistakes rather than the cleverness of her enemy. Time and again Athens is warned to accept just terms and settle the war, but good fortune and mad ambition drive her to seek for more. Instead of seeing her unforeseen successes as due to chance, she assumes they are due to her own strength. So, losing her sense of proportion, she loses a sense of herself and her proper bounds. With terrible irony the message is spelled out at Melos and in the pages that describe the splendor and folly of the Sicilian expedition, "undertaken with hopes for the future which . . . were of the most far-reaching kind" (VI.31; p. 386). Room for maneuver is lost and, with the ascendancy of Alcibiades, all glitter and wild ambition, reason and balance are quite gone. The narrative rolls relentlessly toward that conclusion for which the beginning prepared and which has drawn closer with increasing urgency through the work. For those who love the Athens of Pericles, the inevitable end is unbearable. "This was the greatest Hellenic action that took place during this war, and, in my opinion, the greatest action that we know of in Hellenic history—to the victors the most brilliant of successes, to the vanquished the most calamitous of defeats; for they were utterly and entirely defeated; their sufferings were on an enormous scale; their losses were, as they say, total; army, navy, everything was destroyed, and out of many, only a few returned" (VII.87; p. 488).

So the tragedy ends. Nothing follows by probability or necessity from this point. The work is complete. The emotions of pity and fear have been evoked and purged. Our sense of an ending has been satisfied. But Thucydides adds, "so ended the events in Sicily," and returns to the reaction in Athens and Book VIII. It is a little as though Shakespeare had let Lear live on, and described his later trivial comings and going. If the work might sensibly be read as a tragedy, what can be said in the face of Book VIII and its abrupt and indifferent finish?

It clearly presents a problem, but it is a problem that Thucydides seems to have shared. Book VIII is scrappy and unrevised. It has no *oratio recta* speeches, though there are what appear to be notes for such speeches. We know also that Thucydides was revising and polishing other parts of the work as much as a decade after the events described in Book VIII. So why is it left dangling?

My thesis is not meant to imply that Thucydides is a tragedian and not a historian. My argument is, rather, that in order to make best sense of the *History,* we should be alert to fundamental elements in it that are antihistorical, but which are familiar to us from ancient medicine and tragedy. Yet the work is not a "pure" tragedy either, despite the underlying tragic mythos. Book VIII, and many other elements that are there due to Thucydides' precise, historical inquiry after particulars, disturb the movement of the narrative and interject what Aristotle might call "episodic" sequences of events. These episodes, and some of the irrelevant notes and minor excursuses "succeed one another without probable or necessary sequence" (*Poetics,* IX.10), and interrupt the building of the pure, tragic emotions.[33] (That is, if we wanted to highlight the tragedy, we would edit all kinds of details from the text.) Yet the most central and confident features of the text are those that articulate the tragic mythos or paradigm, whereas those that we would cut in order to improve the tragic effect are those that seem to have been written with a sense of uncertainty and left unrevised—Book VIII being the clearest example. So, whereas the existence of Book VIII is evidence of Thucydides' commitment to more than simply turning the account of Athens' fall into a tragedy, its incomplete and unrevised condition seems to be evidence of its not contributing to his prime purpose, which was to enunciate the universal truth of the tragic nature of human things.

I have tried to indicate why it is sensible to read Thucydides' *History* as a tragedy, albeit a somewhat unusual and imperfect one. In

33. It is, however, noteworthy that these episodic elements decrease as the work moves toward its climax in the harbor at Syracuse. I agree with Westlake's reading that in the second "half" of the work (after V.25) Thucydides "adopted even stricter standards of relevance." See H. D. Westlake, *Essays on the Greek Historians and Greek History* (Manchester: Manchester Univ. Press, 1969), Ch. 1. I think, however, that the standards were derived from his aim to body forth his universal truth even more than from his aim to relate the particular truths of the war.

spirit, it seems to have much more in common with Euripides' work than with that of any historian. Yeats' phrase, "tragedy wrought to its uttermost," seems to characterize the work of both men. Both seem to torture the forms in which they express themselves, striving to set forth completely the truth about human things. I have argued that the *History* continues to fuel controversy because it is a tortured attempt to achieve two ends that we recognize as impossible and mutually incompatible. It strives first to record *wie es eigentlich gewesen war* with complete objectivity, and second to embody that record in a form that shows a universal truth about the way things happen.

One may say that Thucydides "failed" to write a proper history or a proper tragedy, but this is an empty and anachronistic accusation. He has succeeded in writing a unique and uniquely valuable hybrid—a term we can give to it only because of categories established after his time. We tend to read back too much from later categories and distinctions. Hippocrates fits into our category of "medical science" more readily than any other, and so we tend to notice in him only what is relevant to our sense of that category, ignoring everything else as more or less insignificant and anomalous. But what are anomalies to us were quite as significant, and in Hippocrates' case even more significant, than what we recognize as familiar. While there is nothing wrong with highlighting those features that have survived and been built on and that form sometimes the very foundations of our more advanced sciences, it is fallacious to think that this is also an appropriate method for understanding Hippocrates' work.

It is the same with Thucydides. He is, of course, the originator of those elements of historiography that we value most and that we consider the foundation of that method of inquiry. After the myths and travelers' tales, which were about all Thucydides received as accounts of the world around him and its past, the "creator of history would set himself no more ambitious task than to save from the dissolving fabric of human fact a few hard stones, unhewn, and fit only to serve for a foundation" (*Th. Myth.*, p. 76). That the first history was infected with the antihistorical aim of showing an inexorable moral necessity operating in men's affairs should cause no great surprise. The work, after all, sprang not from the mind of Zeus but from that of a cultured Greek at the high point of tragic consciousness.

Kitto, in warning the modern reader against Cornford's interpretation, writes that it is rash to assume "that so strong a writer as Thucydides could not say what he thought and meant without a model."[34] To argue that some paradigm determines the way we see certain things is not to argue that it thereby determines all our thinking. When Cornford claims that Thucydides inherited certain ideas that Aeschylus contributed to the "circumambient atmosphere," he was not claiming, as Kitto seems to assume, that Thucydides "was not thinking for himself."[35] As I indicated above, Cornford suggests that human thinking is always partially determined—at some level the means we use to make sense of things are not themselves open to reflection—and partially free or original. One inherits presuppositions, or a priori forms of thought, and uses these to make sense of the world. Careful observation and some courage might persuade us to undertake the psychologically painful task of abandoning some part of the inherited set of presuppositions and restructuring them better to represent our perception of reality.[36] It suggests a mechanism whereby our minds have gradually become released from the determinism of myth to the relative freedom of rationality. And this has been a gradual process, open to inspection in some degree only in ancient Greek writers and artists. A proper understanding of those few great works that stand at the fountainhead of our traditions of rational inquiry demands a precise appreciation of the degree to which they have freed themselves from mythic determinism.

This seems neither more nor less than the claim Cornford made. Kitto's criticism seems aimed at a straw man. Cornford argues that Thucydides did indeed use ideas learned from Aeschylus in composing his *History,* but this "model" was not, as Kitto seems to imply, at the superficial level of gods and spirits, but rather at the level of what I have called the mythic paradigm of tragedy—for whose form, it seems difficult to deny, Aeschylus was to some degree responsible.

It may be argued that my attempt to rescue Cornford's case has led to a notion of "mythic paradigm"[37] that is so general and vague that

34. Kitto, *Poiesis,* p. 280.
35. Ibid., p. 281.
36. The process of adapting received modes of perception or expression to new requirements is well described in Erich Auerbach's *Mimesis,* trans. Willard Trask (Princeton: Princeton Univ. Press, 1953); E. H. Gombrich's *Art and Illusion* (Princeton: Princeton Univ. Press, 1960); and Bruno Snell's *The Discovery of the Mind,* trans. T. G. Rosenmeyer (Cambridge, Mass.: Harvard Univ. Press, 1953).
37. Clearly, I have borrowed much of the meaning of this term from Thomas S. Kuhn's notion of paradigms that determine aspects of scientific behavior. Kuhn has had to bear much criticism for the vagueness and ambiguity of his use of this term—one critic detecting at least twenty-two different uses—and similar criticisms might justifiably be made against my adaptation of it in this essay. Obviously, I think the notion is fruitful, but it is very difficult to deal clearly and precisely with an area that has hardly hitherto been acknowledged to exist. Nor do we have available a vocabulary rich in distinctions for dealing with the complex and abstract organizing elements in narratives.

one might say such mythic paradigms, or mythoi, underlie all historical narratives simply by virtue of their being coherent compositions of
events. My answer to such criticism would be: "Precisely so." Inevitably, even in the most modern historical monograph, some paradigmatic element will play a determining role in the selection of what
kinds of things will serve as events and in how these elements are
connected, and this paradigm will be as unconscious to the modern
historian as Thucydides' tragic paradigm was to him. It will be so
because it determines, among other things, what is perceived as natural—especially in terms of causal sequences.

The tragic paradigm that determines the relationship among the
main events in Thucydides' *History* determines in some general and
subtle way the nature of causality that operates in the work, that
makes the work "move." It seems to follow from this, and from the
observation that different kinds of paradigms operate in typical modern monographs—and I suggest this tentatively—that causality in historiography is not open to general interpretation. Rather, in each
narrative it is determined by the paradigm or mythos that governs the
total form, that makes it into a whole and a unit. Causality, then,
might seem to be a function of mythos, or paradigm; it is not something "given" and constant in historiography. Thus, attempts to analyze the nature of causality in historiography might better begin by
examining the selection and emplotment of incidents in any given
work, or body of works, rather than from some general model.

In the case of tragedy, the paradigm or mythos is quite stark, and it is
recognized more readily because of its unique effect. But if, for economy's sake only, we accept Frye's progression of modes,[38] we might
consider the dominant mode of modern historiography to be ironic, in
Frye's sense of the term. This ironic mode of perception determines
what we accept as natural in the progression of things in the world, and
in light of it we tend to judge romantic, comic, or tragic causal schemata as false. That is, insofar as Thucydides uses a tragic paradigm, to
that degree we judge that he "falsified" history—because our view is
not tragic but ironic (again, in Frye's sense). Nor is there any apparent
way that we can climb out of all paradigms and declare that one is right,
that one *properly* represents the nature of causality in the world. Paradigms seem to belong to the species of "very general and abstract
metaphor," and as such are not open to the kinds of truth tests applica-
ble to the elements they serve to organize.

38. Northrop Frye, *Anatomy of Criticism: Four Essays* (Princeton: Princeton Univ.
Press, 1957). I say "for economy's sake only" because it seems to me that occasionally
even Frye and more frequently some of his followers have confused the elaboration of
the useful metaphor he developed with a description of reality.

Historical causality, causality in the world, must remain, then, ineffable. General accounts of causality, this suggests, involve what we might call a confusion over where we end and the world begins. That is, there has been a tendency to see as a part of the events of the world what is really a part of the way we make sense of them—historiographical causality. An adequate account of historiographical causality must examine what determines the way in which each work isolates and creates events and accepts as natural a certain kind of causal connection between those events. The prior task—to echo Kermode—is to make sense of the way we make sense of the world. Cornford, despite his rather annoying and misleading superstructure of gods and spirits, seems to have had a fine sense of what we contribute to the knowledge we construct.

Richard Reinitz

4
NIEBUHRIAN IRONY
AND HISTORICAL
INTERPRETATION

The Relationship between Consensus
and New Left History

The most common categories into which historiographers divide works on American history written in the twentieth century are based upon the interpretations of past politics in those works. Progressive historians, scholars such as Charles Beard and Vernon L. Parrington, saw the dominant theme of American history as the conflict between a democratic, agrarian majority and an urban, commercial and industrial elite. In the period following the Second World War, consensus history developed in opposition to the Progressive view. Historians such as Richard Hofstadter and Oscar Handlin argued that the distinctive feature of American history was not conflict but an agreement upon fundamentals which underlay our national political life. During the 1960s, as dissent became increasingly visible, a more critical view of the American past was asserted by a number of younger historians such as Staughton Lynd and Eugene Genovese. Although the interpretations offered by this group of New Left scholars appear more varied (at least from our present perspective) than those of either the Progressive or consensus historians, all of them presented visions of America that can be described as radical.

These politically rooted historiographic categories have proven useful. For one thing they reveal the connection between the writing of history and the climate of opinion in the period in which the history was written. They also provide insight into the social perspectives of historians. The Progressive historians were also political progressives, most of those who wrote consensus history believed in a moderate liberalism, and the New Left historians are more or less identifiable with the political movement of the same name. But these categories can also be misleading if they are applied too rigidly or too generally. Some contemporary historians simply do not fit into either the consensus or New Left groups and there are other ways of classifying many of those who do fit into the two groups. Historians can be grouped by methodology; the use by a historian of quantitative evidence and statistical techniques, for example, tells us nothing about his point of view since these methods are used by some consensus writers as well as by some New Left ones. Distinctions in subject matter are also important. Scholars who write the new social history often have New Left views, but some of them suggest consensus interpretations.

All of these categories have been discussed by other historiographers.[1] I would like to propose another way of classifying contemporary historians, one based upon a literary analysis of their works. In spite of some persuasive calls for the literary criticism of historical writing, American historiographers have made few efforts to deal with the craft in those terms.[2] Much more attention has been paid to the substantive interpretations present in works of history and to the methods of collecting and analyzing information used in them than to the forms in which they are written. Yet most historians are unwilling to abandon the ancient claim that history is a form of literature. More significantly, as literate human beings many historians recognize how much the substance of a written work is shaped by the form in which it is conveyed, although they are reluctant to apply that recognition to their understanding of written history.

In this essay I shall examine one aspect of the formal structure of some of the writings of four major contemporary historians in order to

1. The best general guide to twentieth-century American historiography is John Higham, particularly Higham et al., *History: The Development of Historical Studies in the United States* (Englewood Cliffs, N. J.: Prentice-Hall, 1965), and the essays collected in his *Writing American History* (Bloomington: Indiana Univ. Press, 1970). See Robert Allen Skotheim, ed., *The Historian and the Climate of Opinion* (Reading, Mass.: Addison-Wesley, 1969) for a demonstration of how effectively the writing of American history can be organized in terms of its relationship to changes in the spirit of the age. Robert F. Berkhofer, Jr., has recently argued that the most fundamental transformation of historical interpretations in the last decade is the result of a methodological shift from a cultural to a social focus; see "Clio and the Culture Concept: Some Impressions of a Changing Relationship in American Historiography," *Social Science Quarterly,* 53 (1972), 297–320.

2. Both the most persuasive calls for, and best examples of, the literary and conceptual criticism of American historical writing have come from David Levin and Gene Wise. See Levin's "The Literary Criticism of History," in *In Defense of Historical Literature* (New York: Hill and Wang, 1967), pp. 1–33, and *History as Romantic Art* (Stanford: Stanford Univ. Press, 1959), and Wise's *American Historical Explanations* (Homewood, Ill.: Dorsey, 1973).

show how even a limited literary analysis can change our perceptions of the interpretative significance of works of history. My concern here is exclusively with the presence or absence of a specific kind of irony. In no sense is this intended to be a full critique of these works. They will be compared to a particular form but their style, their rhetorical mode, and even other aspects of their structures will not be studied.

The ironic pattern to which I will compare these histories is derived from Reinhold Neibuhr. We perceive a human action as ironic, in the sense in which I will use the term, when we see the consequences of that action as contrary to the original intention of the actor and can locate a significant part of the reason for the discrepancy in the actor himself or his intention.[3] This kind of irony is distinguished from other meanings of that protean term by its moral seriousness. It has no necessary relationship to the most common definition of irony, which refers to the rhetorical devices by which a writer or speaker signals that he means the opposite of what he appears to say. Neither does Niebuhrian irony imply the determinism suggested by the cliché "the irony of fate," nor does it have the connotations of contempt or superiority which are characteristically suggested by some other forms of irony.[4]

Niebuhrian irony, like other literary forms used in the writing of history, is a device for drawing some aspects of the past to the center of our awareness while leaving others in obscurity. It implies a certain kind of human world, one in which people are free to act but not so free or powerful as to be able to control the consequences of their actions consistently. Historical events are the product of human action and the result of human intention but not the unmitigated realization of those intentions. People perceived ironically are complex and contradictory creatures. Their virtues are seen as linked to their faults and their weaknesses to their strengths. The reasons why their ac-

3. See Reinhold Niebuhr, *The Irony of American History* (New York: Scribner's, 1952); Wise, *American Historical Explanations;* and Wise, "Implicit Irony in Perry Miller's *New England Mind,"* *Journal of the History of Ideas,* 29 (1968), 579–600. My definition is a slight modification of Wise's.

4. Some of these distinctions are discussed in Douglas C. Muecke, *The Compass of Irony* (London: Methuen, 1969); A. E. Dyson, *The Crazy Fabric: Essays in Irony* (New York: St. Martin's, 1965); Bert O. States, *Irony and Drama* (Ithaca: Cornell Univ. Press, 1971), pp. 3, 14; Kenneth Burke, *A Grammar of Motives* (New York: Prentice-Hall, 1945), pp. 514, 515; and Northrop Frye, *Anatomy of Criticism: Four Essays* (Princeton: Princeton Univ. Press, 1957), pp. 34, 237. Hayden White has recently analyzed the fundamental implications of rhetorical irony as one of the basic poetic modes that shape historical works in his highly innovative *Metahistory: The Historical Imagination in Nineteenth-Century Europe* (Baltimore: Johns Hopkins Univ. Press, 1973).

tions often do not produce the intended results are generally to be found in the illusions about themselves and the world and the comforting pretensions to innocence, power, virtue, and wisdom from which they suffer. Moral responsibility is real but in part unconscious because of these illusions and pretensions. The function of the ironic historian is in part therapeutic; he seeks to expose those illusions and pretensions as products of the past and so to free people to act responsibly and consciously in the present. If people are made aware of the irony of their actions they are liberated from the compulsion to go on acting ironically. In order to write effective therapeutic history a historian must assume an attitude toward his subjects that combines criticism of their faults with recognition of their virtues. All of this suggests how great a difference the presence or absence of Niebuhrian irony can make in a historical work. It is related to the pictures of humankind and the historical process suggested by a historian, to the image conveyed of the particular people studied, and to the function assumed for his own writing. To know whether or not irony is used in a particular historical work may tell us more about the significance of the historical interpretation it presents than does knowledge of the political category into which the historian can be placed.

Louis Hartz and Daniel J. Boorstin are generally classified as consensus historians. They are, indeed, among the most important of the scholars in that category.[5] William A. Williams and Gabriel Kolko are both leading New Left historians. Since New Left history is less sharply delineated than consensus history there are substantial differences between Williams and Kolko, but they both clearly belong in that group. It is difficult to imagine a definition of New Left history that would make much sense if it excluded Williams or Kolko. Their contributions have been so great that the category would be greatly diminished if either of them was absent from it.[6] By examining the extent to which the ironic pattern can be found in the works of these historians, unexpected resemblances and contrasts can be exposed. Those who use Niebuhrian irony—Hartz and Williams—offer us remarkably comparable visions of humanity, of history, and of Amer-

5. Richard Hofstadter referred to Hartz and Boorstin as "the two leading consensus theorists" in *The Progressive Historians* (New York: Knopf, 1968) p. 444. They are repeatedly used as outstanding examples of historians of that school. See for example Marian J. Morton, *The Terrors of Ideological Politics: Liberal Historians in a Conservative Mood* (Cleveland: Press of Case Western Reserve Univ., 1972), and Skotheim, ed., *Historian and Opinion*.

6. On New Left history see Irwin Unger, "The 'New Left' and American History: Some Recent Trends in United States Historiography," *American Historical Review*, 72 (1967), 1237–63.

ica. I shall argue, in fact, that they are more similar to each other as historians than Hartz is to Boorstin or Williams to Kolko in spite of the political categorization of their works.

I

Louis Hartz has been one of the most influential of those historians who have presented comprehensive interpretations of American history in terms of consensus and continuity. The broad outlines of Hartz's vision of the American past are familiar to all historians. He argues that liberalism has been the unrecognized and unchallenged master of American political thought, the basis of our politics on which there was a general but unconscious agreement. In contrast to the situation in Europe, American liberalism had no competition from either the Right or the Left. "European liberalism, because it was cursed with feudalism, was forced to create the mentality of socialism, and thus was twice cursed. American liberalism, freed of the one was freed of the other, and hence was twice blessed."[7] As a result the history of the United States was the product of the development of the implications of liberalism, developments which took place in isolation from other political forces.

Hartz's version of consensus history is far from uncritical of America. He maintains that the fact that American political conflict has taken place within a limited range of opinion does not mean that conflict has not been bitter. American political leaders have not generally recognized the agreement upon fundamentals which they share. They have been victims of the limitations of their situation which prevented them from seeing other, deeper, contrasts and so recognizing what they have in common with their opponents. Hartz refers repeatedly to the "absolutism" of American liberalism, which has "the sober faith that its norms are self-evident. It is one of the most powerful absolutisms in the world." The American faith in liberalism has been irrational, "so irrational that it has not even been recognized for what it is: liberalism" (pp. 58, 10, 11). Hartz emphasizes the dangers which liberal absolutism, irrationality, and unconsciousness pose for both domestic civil liberties and a rational foreign policy.

The central theme of Hartz's account of the development of American politics and political thought fits the ironic form. That development involves the evolution of liberalism from high Whiggery to de-

---

7. Hartz, *The Liberal Tradition in America: An Interpretation of American Political Thought since the Revolution* (New York: Harcourt, Brace & World, 1955), p. 78. Subsequent references to this work appear in the text.

mocracy and the subsequent interaction of two kinds of liberals, Whigs and democrats. In Hartz's account of that evolution, the Whigs and the democrats are seen as successively contributing each to his own defeat in a twofold ironic pattern. The very manner in which the Whigs, as Federalists, secured the acceptance of the Constitution prepared the way for their eventual replacement by democrats: "For the very solidarity which supported the Constitution meant that Whig elitism would be isolated as the democratic tide of the nation asserted itself once more . . . . In this sense the mistaken views of American life that the Whigs cherished cost them heavily" (p. 86). The Whigs perceived America as if it were Europe and attacked the democrats as if they were European radicals leading a mob. This "conservative denunciation of the people not only becomes suicidal, since it is precisely the people who are sure to shatter them, but loses much of its connection to reality" (p. 93). Hartz makes it very clear that in his view the Whigs were largely responsible for their own defeat. "American Whiggery, had it not been strategically paralyzed over most of its early history, had it not had an impulse to duplicate European patterns, . . . could have avoided all of this" (p. 94). The Whigs could have adopted a different strategy, one suited to American and not European conditions. Eventually the Whigs were able to do this and to regain power by adopting the Horatio Alger myth that all Americans could be capitalists: "This was the law of Whig compensation inherent in American life" (p. 112).

The irony of the American Whig is intertwined with that of the American democrat. The latter's popularity stemmed in part from his ability to attack the Whig as an aristocrat, ignoring the extent to which in America both Whigs and democrats were liberals, and obscuring those of his own characteristics that would in the end make him vulnerable to the Whig as Horatio Alger capitalist: "Above all, the historic petit-bourgeois dilemmas of the Western world remained: individualist fear despite a faith in the majority, capitalist hunger despite talk of 'monopoly.' These drives, as we know, ultimately enchained the American democrat to the very Whigs he was able to shatter in 1800 and 1828 . . . . The American democratic giant bought his strength at the price of weakness, his power to defeat Whiggery at the price of losing to it in the end. Here was America's law of Whig compensation mirrored in reverse." The American democrat "is too thoroughly torn by inner doubt, too constantly in danger of selling out to his opponent, for a warrior legend ever successfully to be built around him"; he is "a Hercules with the brain of a Hamlet" (p. 119). An illustration of the inward confusions and self-contradictions of the democrat was his attitude toward the use of state power for the regulation of economic activity. He made an early "identification of the 'capitalist' and the 'aristocrat' with the public action of legislatures" (p. 136). This stance became awkward for him, "for when he himself began to adopt large parts of the Whig program, he was put in the position of grinding out the very demons who oppressed him. This is the awful irony that cuts through the career of the American democrat from the time of Jefferson onward" (p. 137).

The interlocking drama of American Whigs and democrats underlies Hartz's conception of consensus politics in America. In language strongly suggestive of Niebuhrian irony he characterizes his "central point: The weakness of the American democrat was a part of his strength, his defeat a part of his victory" (p. 139). Hartz describes how in the era following the Civil War the Whigs reversed their position on state economic action and adopted the laissez-faire policies which the antebellum democrats had succeeded in identifying with Americanism, using "the ancient arguments of the American democrat himself" (p. 216). (Hartz's comments in this connection point out how the appropriation of laissez-faire policies by those who possess economic power in America was possible because of the failure of Americans to recognize the realities of such forms of power.) The ironies of the interchange between right- and left-wing liberals continues in the twentieth century in various Progressive movements; it can be seen "in the imperfect knowledge they have of the enemy they face, above all in their failure to see their own unwitting contribution to his strength" (p. 13).

Hartz is very concerned with the idea that American history has involved a flight from confrontation with social issues and an escape from the complexities characteristic of Europe. In the mid-twentieth century "modern America finds itself in the big wide world while the Founding fathers managed to escape from it." America has a "tradition of escape itself, of a nonrevolutionary nation as compared with a Europe that has emerged out of revolution and an Asia that is now undergoing it" (p. 284). When confronted with the non-American world, American escapism may be followed by an equally dangerous tendency to try to change that world. "Americans seem to oscillate between fleeing from the rest of the world and embracing it with too ardent a passion. An absolute national morality is inspired either to withdraw from 'alien' things or to transform them: it cannot live comfortably by their side" (p. 286).

Hartz's discussion of the history of American foreign relations has the therapeutic purpose of showing the need to overcome our tendencies to continue to escape from the world and to perceive it only through the prism of our own peculiar experience. We must allow an awareness of other peoples to inform our sense of ourselves if we are to overcome our narrow absolutist liberalism, our "Americanism," in a process analogous to the development of an ironic historical consciousness. In a penetrating ironic comment Hartz points out how our increased involvement with the rest of mankind in the twentieth century is at once a major source of our problems, or of the increase of already existing problems, and our only hope for overcoming them.

> For if that involvement intensifies nationalist blindness in some, it serves to educate others . . . . There has been, in other words, throughout the twentieth century an impulse to transcend the American perspective evoked by the very clash of cultures which has closed it down, and as the case of Wilson shows, the two tendencies have usually fought it out within a single American mind. "Americanism" is at once heightened and shattered by the crashing impact of the rest of the world upon it. And so, curiously enough, the answer to the national blindness that the new time produces is the national enlightenment that it also produces: the race between the two is a fateful one indeed. Which is to say that America must look to its contact with other nations to provide that spark of philosophy, that grain of relative insight that its own history has denied it. (p. 287)

This call for America to become conscious of the limits of "Americanism" through comparative self-understanding induced by world contact is very similar to the idea of ironic historical consciousness freeing America from the illusions that lead us to go on acting ironically. This therapeutic idea is carried into a more explicitly comparative framework and given a clearer historical dimension in Hartz's later book, *The Founding of New Societies* (1964), an even broader work than *The Liberal Tradition*. In it Hartz treats the United States and the other colonial areas as offshoots (he calls them "fragments") of Europe. As such they take on the character of the historical force that was dominant in their founding: for example, French Canada, feudalism; the United States, bourgeois liberalism or "whiggism"; Australia, working-class radicalism. The subsequent development of the fragments differs from that of Europe because the colonies lack the complexity of conflicting classes and historical forces that arise in Europe after they are founded. Instead, the history of the fragments is governed by the working out of the internal logic of the one major stream that controlled their initiation. In this context "liberal absolutism"—"Americanism" in the earlier book—becomes a form of "fragment consciousness," a consciousness marked by the effort to forget its cosmopolitan origins. Hartz seeks to overcome our forgetfulness, to expose the fact that America is merely a fragment, and perhaps to undo the fragmentary character of American consciousness by that exposure.

The theme of American escapism, which Hartz began to develop in *The Liberal Tradition,* is integrally and ironically involved in his new fragmentation theory. In the twentieth century America has placed itself in a position where it must face in the rest of the world the very social conflicts that it sought to flee. "The fragments . . . are involved . . . in one of the strangest issues of change that the world impact of the modern era has produced. For it is the irony of that impact that it has hurled back at the fragments, after centuries and from wholly unexpected angles, the very Western revolution they originally fled. Their escape has turned out to be an illusion."[8] It was one of the major strengths of the fragment (as well as the source of the absolutism of its liberalism) that it provided its citizens with a world view that allowed them to forget that they were a fragment of a larger whole. This lack of consciousness of its fragmentary character "is the reason for the peculiar trauma of the fragment as it is suddenly forced back, through the world events of our time, into the context of revolution. It does not return as an ideology. It returns as a world, a nation, as a way of racial life" (p. 20). The world revolution of our time is inescapable. "We can see now, with a kind of sudden Hegelian retrospect, that inherent in the whole legendary process of 'escape' from Europe there were mechanisms canceling out its results . . . . As the globe contracted, the Western revolution that the fragments escaped was spreading through it with increasing rapidity, so that ultimately it was bound to overtake them from a distant place suddenly made near. If Holland was left behind, there was still Russia, China, the awakening states of Africa" (pp. 20–21). To the extent that the fragments rely upon the mechanisms that had worked for them before, their response is inappropriate to the situation, in a typically ironic pattern.

More painful to the people of the fragment than even the discovery that the world revolution moves in directions that cancel out their escape is the response of their own young to those changes. This irony is one that was visible in 1964 in ways that it had not been in 1955. The sons and daughter of the liberal fragment "will reject the proposition that 'Americanism' is the instinctive emotion of all hu-

8. Hartz, *The Founding of New Societies* (New York: Harcourt, Brace & World, 1964), p. 3. Subsequent references to this work appear in the text.

manity . . . . Indeed they will go a step farther. They will recapture the memory of Europe itself, and in the very teeth of the fragment hysteric, they will expose the relativity of . . . its ethic. They will announce outright that the fragment is a 'fragment' " (p. 22). "The fragment world passes, destroyed by the same 'honest' response to experience which created it." (p. 23).

The fragment character of America produced a specific blindness to that which we most need to understand in the present world: the attraction of collectivism in its communist form. In this book as in the earlier one Hartz writes of one feature of our experience, "of social-ism fading in America because feudalism has been left behind," as a source of great strength (p. 7). But that source of strength in contem-porary times has become a source of weakness.

> The United States and the other modern fragments . . . are destined to deal with a world they cannot out of their own experience understand and for which they cannot out of their experience prescribe. That world . . . must achieve modernity through methods other than the Mayflower voyage. Extremisms of right and left offer such methods, and for that reason the struggle against them by the Enlightenment fragments calls for a leap of the imagination outside their own experi-ence. But that leap is as difficult as any that could be made in the realm of domestic social policy. (p. 46)

The most important advance in *The Founding of New Societies* over *The Liberal Tradition* is in the expansion of Hartz's concept of the function of historical consciousness, an advance that brings his later work closer to the hope that through ironic awareness people may be freed from the illusions and the compulsive limits that their historical experience imposes on their thought. Hartz finds in the contemporary world an expansion of consciousness within the frag-ments, a breaking up of their narrow vision. "The exposure of the fragment universe by the world impact of the present time, reversing the history of the fragment, is bound to be traumatic. But it brings with it a moral liberation, an enlargement of consciousness, which for its own sake would well be worth the struggle" (p. 23). Hartz argues that the fragment-comparative approach to history can itself contri-bute to that enlargement of consciousness. He asks: "Is not compari-son the true historical 'experiment?' In American historical work, . . . we have spoken much of 'objectivity.' But this concern has actually masked the deeper plunging of historical study into the frag-ment interior. The theory of the fragment, at the very moment that it illuminates our national dilemmas, promises in a new sense the fulfillment of that 'objectivity' . . . . It is the Hegelian virtue of our necessity that the difficulty of the present time drives us toward a new enlightenment'' (pp. 121, 122). To enlarge our consciousness beyond the limitations of the fragment we must develop a historical awareness of the fact that we are a fragment. Only knowledge of our fragmented character can enable us to transcend it. Only knowledge of irony can free us from irony.

The conjunction between Hartz's vision of American history and the ironic pattern is obvious. Whigs and democrats in turn defeat themselves repeatedly because of illusions about their own nature and that of their opponents. Flight from European revolution and conflict was one of the roots of American strength, but because of that escape and that strength, in the twentieth century America faces the rest of the world crippled by illusions of uniqueness which prevent us from dealing realistically with other nations. As we act on the world stage we tend to assume, in our blindness to our character as a fragment, that all other people are like ourselves. Above all, Hartz's conception of the function of historical understanding fits the Niebuhrian model. A comparative and cosmopolitan consciousness may overcome our ''forgetfulness'' and may free us from the pretensions that lead us to continue to act so as to bring about results contrary to our intentions. For Hartz, human beings are self-contradictory creatures—Americans, whose virtues are linked to their faults, no less than others. American history is largely a story of unintended consequences into which our own illusions have led us, and the ironic study of that history offers the possibility of a therapeutic dispelling of those illusions. Although Hartz certainly is a consensus historian, it seems clear that we can see more deeply into the implications of his work if we also perceive it as, in literary terms, permeated by Niebuhrian irony. Examined from this angle, his vision of America and his conception of the function of historical knowledge have more in common with those of a radical historian like Williams than with another consensus historian like Boorstin.

II

Daniel J. Boorstin might be regarded as the archetypal consensus historian, particularly in his most general statement about the American past, *The Genius of American Politics*. He emphatically insists that the vast majority of Americans share the same fundamental political beliefs. ''Here the number of people who do not accept the predominant values of our society is negligible. Politics here has therefore seldom, if ever, been the realm of ends . . . . However crudely or unsuccessfully articulated, the ends of society in America have nevertheless been generally agreed upon."[9]

Boorstin's central argument in this book is that Americans have failed to produce significant theory, that our agreement upon fundamentals has made it unnecessary for us to develop political philosophy in the way in which Europeans have. Instead of political theory we have had what Boorstin calls a sense of givenness. " 'Givenness' is the belief that values in America are in some way or other automatically defined: given by certain facts of geography or history peculiar to us" (p. 9). He recognizes, and emphasizes, that this concept of givenness amounts to the argument that Americans have believed that they could find the normative in the descriptive. He speaks of "the recurrent tendency in American history to identify the 'is' with the 'ought,' to think of values and a theory of society as implicit in facts about society" (p. 132).[10]

This vision of America is profoundly non-ironic, even anti-ironic. Much of what Boorstin writes in *The Genius of American Politics* sounds like irony, but the essential element is missing: a critical focus on how illusions have led Americans to act so as to contradict their intentions. When Boorstin does perceive moral responsibility in historical actors whose behavior might be understood ironically, he generally suggests that they do not really belong in the American tradition, that they are uncharacteristic. The abolitionists, for example, are presented as "absolutist and abstract." In Boorstin's account, when they based their case on the assertion "that slavery was a moral evil" they could be regarded as setting in motion a possible ironic pattern, but he treats the abolitionists as atypical and relatively unim-

9. Boorstin, *The Genius of American Politics* (Chicago: Univ. of Chicago Press, 1953), pp. 138, 139. Subsequent reference to this work appear in the text. My analysis of Boorstin is based primarily on this book, as it seems to be the most general statement of his consensus interpretation. J. R. Pole emphasizes the importance of it among Boorstin's works, referring to it as "a book that stands as a landmark in his thought and influence" ("Daniel J. Boorstin," in Marcus Cunliffe and Robin W. Winks, eds., *Pastmasters* [New York: Harper & Row, 1969], p. 220). Pole's essay offers sympathetic but critical insights into Boorstin's accomplishments.

10. In two brilliant articles John P. Diggins has explored the philosophical implications of Boorstin's concept of givenness and has revealed its weaknesses as an interpretation of American history. I have found his work most helpful in my effort to understand the relationship between Boorstin's history and irony. See Diggins, "Consciousness and Ideology in American History: The Burden of Daniel J. Boorstin," *American Historical Review*, 76 (1971), 99–118, and "The Perils of Naturalism: Some Reflections on Daniel J. Boorstin's approach to American History," *American Quarterly*, 23 (1971), 153–80.

portant, as outside the mainstream of American history (p. 111).[11] Their potential irony merely serves to confirm his tendency not to see America as ironic.

Boorstin also finds irony in the way in which Europeans, such as the seventeenth-century Puritans, were changed into Americans in spite of their intentions when they settled here—in how "dreams made in Europe—the dreams of the zionist, the perfectionist, the philanthropist, and the transplanter—were dissipated or transformed by the American reality."[12] In *The Genius of American Politics* Boorstin presents the original Puritans as people of high expectations who came to America planning to build a particular type of godly community. They did not fit at all into his vision of what it meant to be American. "Of all people in modern history, these early Puritans could be least accused of confusion about their ends or of that inarticulateness which I have described as a characteristic of American political thought" (p. 37). Significantly, he notes "that Puritanism was a European product, brought here in its nearly finished state" (p. 38).

Boorstin's account of what happened to the Puritans after they came to America is primarily a story of religious declension. The conditions of the New World, aided by some of the traits of the Puritans themselves, made them into Americans. At one point he explicitly refers to this process as ironic, using the term in its Niebuhrian sense.

> A distinctive and paradoxical feature of the American story was that the decline actually came in part from the removal of many of those perils which had earlier confirmed the Puritans' dogmas. The more secure the Puritans became on this continent, the more meager and unimpressive became the daily proofs of their dogma. At the same time,

11. Boorstin's sympathetic treatment of Nat Turner in *The Americans: The National Experience* (New York: Random House, 1965), pp. 183–85, contrasts with his critical attitude toward the abolitionists.

12. Boorstin, *The Americans: The Colonial Experience* (New York: Random House, 1958), p. 1. Subsequent references to this work appear in the text. This quote is characteristic of Boorstin's view in this book of the origins of those American colonies that were either planned in Europe or led by men who sought to build a particular kind of religious community. In his account the Quakers behaved ironically in that their ridigity led them to renounce power and influence in America. Because of this, in Boorstin's view, they lie outside the American mainstream and their ironic behavior is not characteristic of Americans (pp. 35–69). His description of the founding of Georgia can also be understood ironically, but the ironic behavior is that of the English philanthropists who tried to organize the colony from England. The settlers of Georgia themselves became Americans, adapting to the environment and not behaving ironically (pp. 71–96).

> success nourished their pride and gave them a community to which they
> could point as the embodiment of their philosophy. In all this we shall see
> how the New England story re-enacted one of the familiar ironies of
> history: in the very act of establishing their community, they undermined
> the philosophy on which it was to have been founded. (p. 53)

By being successful in America the Puritan ceased in important ways
to be Puritan. He was transformed into an American, a creature who
had some of the features of the Puritan but not his commitments.

More is involved in Boorstin's ironic account of Puritan history
than the mutation of a people with an articulate and deep commitment
to transcendental values into Americans, a people who feel that their
values have been given to them by their environment. Boorstin is also
describing the transformation of a people with the aspirations, expectations, and illusions that produce ironic action into a people who do
not behave ironically because they seek only to do that which can be
done. Irony flows from the perception of a disjunction between human aspiration and what it is possible for human beings actually to
do. It is directly dependent upon a sense of the discrepancy between
the "is" and the "ought." If, as Boorstin argues, Americans are a
people for whom the "is" and the "ought" are blended, then they are
a people who do not behave ironically. In becoming Americans, by
his account, the Puritans lost those characteristics—their sense of
mission, of being called by God to establish in the world a kind of
community that had not previously existed; their aspirations and values, which extended beyond the given—which made them tend to act
ironically. Irony, for Boorstin, then, is clearly un-American. It is
something to which Europeans, with their ideologies, utopias, and
reformations, are subject. In becoming American the Puritans ceased
to be European and thus ceased to be potential ironic actors. The
effect of Boorstin's ironic account of the history of the New England
Puritans is to read irony out of American history.[13]

13. The implications of Boorstin's interpretation are directly contrary to those of
some other historians who perceive the history of the New England Puritans ironically. Perry Miller, for example, also finds the Americanization of the New England
settlers to have been the unintended consequence of some aspects of their own religion, but he does not equate being American with being nonironic. Rather, he conceives the Puritan legacy to America to be in part precisely those heightened expectations and illusions of uniqueness that induce ironic behavior. For Miller, in contrast to
Boorstin, irony is charateristically American. On Miller's ironic account of Puritanism
see Wise, "Implicit Irony," and Wise's *American Historical Explanations,* pp. 315–
43. In Miller's own works, that account can be most clearly seen in *The New England
Mind: From Colony to Province* (Cambridge, Mass.: Harvard Univ. Press, 1953) and

None of this should be surprising. The concepts that Boorstin finds most fundamentally characteristic of America are deeply incompatible with irony. His basic idea of "givenness" collapses the distinction between values and realities, making irony impossible; it denies the contradiction between human aspirations and the circumstances under which people live. As John Diggins has observed: "One finds in *The Genius of American Politics*, and in many of Boorstin's other works, no wise and courageous losers, no agonizing second thoughts about might-have-beens, no brooding over historical alternatives to the given. What happened, happened; those who survived, survived."[14] When Boorstin describes America as a land in which the " 'is' and the 'ought,' the world of fact and the world of fancy, of science and of morals" (*Genius*, p. 175) collapse into one another, he is in effect asserting that the tensions in the general human condition between aspiration and realization, between hope and fulfillment, do not apply to Americans. Niebuhrian irony requires those tensions. To say that we do not suffer them is tantamount to saying that we are a people who do not experience irony.

Boorstin repeatedly and explicitly affirms this view of America as a land in which men do not pursue realizable dreams. He argues that American aspirations have been shaped by what it was possible to do in America, that they did not run beyond the limits of the possible, that it has been the very extent of those possibilities, the richness of opportunity in America, which have made Americans cease to be dreamers like Europeans. "Political dreamers in Europe in the eighteenth and nineteenth centuries *had* to lead a rich fantasy life, precisely because their *real* political life was so frustrating. But America was the land of dreams-come-true; for the oppressed European, life in America was itself fantasy. It was not necessary here to develop theory to prove that man could begin anew, that decent community was possible; life in America seemed itself sufficient proof" (p. 171). Boorstin implicitly denies that Americans suffer from exaggerated expectations, like all other human begins, when he claims that "what

---

the title essay in *Errand into the Wilderness* (New York: Harper & Row, 1956). Sacvan Bercovitch, whose ironic interpretation of the Puritans is similar to Miller's, analyzes the persistence of Puritan rhetorical forms, which foster ironic behavior in later America, in "Horologicals to Chronometricals," in *Literary Monographs*, ed. Eric Rothstein, Vol. 3 (Madison: Univ. of Wisconsin Press, 1970). For a clearly ironic interpretation of American Puritanism by a social historian see Kenneth Lockridge, *A New England Town: The First Hundred Years* (New York: Norton, 1970).

14. Diggins, "Consciousness and Ideology," p. 102.

one *could* build on this continent tended to become the criterion of what one ought to build here'' (p. 161). Rather than a land of heightened expectations, for Boorstin, America is the country of chastened dreams, disillusioned and realistic. Without illusions and aspirations irony is impossible.

In general, then, *The Genius of American Politics* is a book that has the effect of denying the possibility that America can be understood ironically. When Americans seem to have aspirations that would tend to make them ironic actors, Boorstin reads them out of the American tradition. The Puritans enter that tradition only by ceasing to have the goals and values that characterized them as Puritans to begin with. Boorstin's basic categories are set up so as to exclude irony. Givenness denies the fundamental human conflict between values and expectations on the one hand, and the circumstances under which men act and the actual consequences of their actions on the other. He explicitly denies that America is a land of dreamers, of men of high aspiration. This denial is given plausibility by his focus upon political theory, an area within which it makes sense to claim that Americans have been highly pragmatic and traditional. But by that focus he draws our attention away from the factors in American life—the very possibilities and opportunities that Boorstin celebrates—which have encouraged high expectations, expectations which have frequently outrun the possibilities. All in all it is hard to imagine an interpretation of American history further removed from Niebuhrian irony than that of Daniel Boorstin.

It is no accident that the book which presents this extraordinarily nonironic interpretation also contains a conservative and extreme version of consensus history. Boorstin's purpose is to reveal American uniqueness and virtue. His approach is explicitly uncritical. Like all consensus historians he emphasizes the role of continuity and fundamental agreement in American political development. Unlike some others, such as Hartz, he regards these characteristics as unalloyed virtues and turns away from any formulation of his own concepts as critical tools, as when he denies that our lack of political theory is ''a refusal of American statesmen to confront their basic philosophical problems'' (p. 95) and when he urges us not to try to unravel the meaning of our basic agreement because such an effort might produce conflict rather than more agreement (p. 169). Although *The Genius of American Politics* is an interesting and stimulating book, written in a style which few historians can equal, and however understandable Boorstin's defensive posture is in light of the cold war conditions under which he wrote the book, it does homogenize our past, blurring whatever real political and social conflict has existed as well as the more fundamental distinction between values and actualities. It is conservative not only in that it advocates respect for traditions, but also more fundamentally in that its logic requires us to renounce the possibility of human effectiveness in history. It is apologetic not only in the sense that it praises the unalloyed virtues of American pragmatism; it focuses on American uniqueness to the point where our participation in common humanity is obscured.

Boorstin's vision of the United States is too committed to our virtues and our uniqueness to have the distance required for irony. His conception of the function of history is diametrically opposed to that of an ironic historian. For such a scholar, history can be a way to free human beings from the compulsion to repeat ironic patterns by exposing the illusions that led them to act so as to contradict their own intentions. Boorstin not only denies the existence of such illusions and contradictions in America; in effect he urges scholars to refrain from exposing whatever contradictions and illusions there are. The task he sets for himself as a historian—and performs with consummate skill—is the articulation of the myths that he feels underlie American virtues. This is in direct contrast to Hartz, whose ironic version of consensus history is presented in a comparative framework so as to expose the limits of American self-perceptions through contrasts with other countries and the use of external perspectives. Boorstin does make a number of comparative statements, but they all serve to reinforce the legitimacy and value of the belief in givenness, which he maintains distinguishes America from Europe. Comparison serves Boorstin only as a way of reinforcing his conviction of American uniqueness, not as a means of locating our distinctiveness in relation to that of other nations, of placing us in a context in which the ways that we are similar to them are clarified along with the ways in which we differ from them. In general, his history is explicitly and deliberately uncritical.

The differences irony reveals between Hartz and Boorstin suggest how powerful a tool of historiographic analysis such a literary concept can be. Both of these historians belong in the same substantive category; they both see American history as characterized by an agreement upon fundamentals, but by comparing their two versions of that interpretation to the ironic pattern it becomes clear how radically different are their implications. Boorstin offers a picture of the American as a truly pragmatic creature, free of inner contradictions and directly and realistically responsive to the environment and opportunity. For him, as people become American they cease to have those traits that lead them to act ironically. Hartz perceives Americans to be as complex as other people. For Boorstin, America possesses unique and unmixed virtues; for Hartz the virtues that America does possess are linked to evil. In a direct contradiction, Boorstin's concept of givenness can be seen as an expression of that very "forgetfulness" and escapism which Hartz seeks to expose and transcend. For Boorstin, Americans are free of ideology; for Hartz the belief that we have no ideology is an illusion of innocence generated by our absolute commitment to the ideology of liberalism. Both Boorstin and Hartz imply a democratic America in the sense that for them the vast majority of the people are involved in the nation, but Boorstin's Americans are innocent because he sees no major national sin, whereas Hartz's ironic perception exposes guilt and the evil that may arise out of America's blind righteousness. The purpose of *The Genius of American Politics* is to remind us of our unique virtues. Hartz conceives of the writing of history as ironic therapy; he wishes to expose the pretensions of American uniqueness, to generate a comparative and ironic consciousness of the limitations of American liberal absolutism so that we shall be free to transcend it.

III

William Appleman Williams is the senior historian among those generally categorized as New Left. His work as a whole conveys a vision of America that is highly compatible with irony. The center of that vision is the recognition of the way in which Americans have characteristically avoided confronting internal social problems by trying to expand the area of our national market. Developed in response to the frontier situation, this mode of behavior is seen by Williams as continuing while America became more involved with the world beyond the continent toward the end of the last century. Expansion for Williams was not simply the result of the narrow self-interest of an American elite, but arose out of the aspirations and even ideals of the majority of Americans, particularly the farmers who represent for him the best of the nation. Suffering from the illusion that the long-run solution to their economic difficulties lay in expansion and the presumption that other peoples could best realize their own destiny by becoming like us, Americans came to support a policy of imperialism, which has led the nation into grave difficulties. The essential elements of irony can be seen in this vision, in spite of the abstraction of Williams' language, which, like that of Hartz, sometimes obscures the perception of irony. For Williams, as for Hartz, Americans are self-

contradictory creatures who act so as to produce unintended consequences because of the illusions and pretensions from which they
suffer. Their virtues are linked to their faults as they relate to the rest
of the world with a generosity that would impose those virtues on
others. In contrast to some other New Left writers, he clearly sees
the American people, as a whole, involved in our national policy.
Most significantly, like Hartz, Williams conceives of history as a
therapeutic enterprise, one that may help to free us from the illusions
and pretensions that lead us to continue to act ironically.

Williams writes more explicitly about tragedy than about irony,
particularly in his *Tragedy of American Diplomacy,* but by tragedy he
means something very similar to Niebuhrian irony. For Williams,
American tragedy did not flow from the deliberate choice of evil by
American leaders but rather was the unintended consequence of actions undertaken out of divided motives. Referring to American policy toward Cuba in the late 1890s, Williams writes:

> American leaders were not evil men. They did not conceive and exe-
> cute some dreadful conspiracy. Nor were they treacherous hypocrites.
> They believed deeply in the ideals they proclaimed . . . .
>
> Precisely for those reasons, however, American diplomacy contained
> the fundamental elements of tragedy. It held within itself, that is to say,
> several contradictory truths. Those truths, left to follow out their given
> logic without modification by men who understood that process and
> acted on their knowledge, would ultimately clash in a devastating up-
> heaval and crisis.[15]

Implicitly Williams suggests that Americans are responsible for the
tragic outcome of their policies not because Americans are evil but
because they are unconscious of the contradictions among the
"truths" to which they are committed. Such a vision of the tragic is
very close to the Niebuhrian conception of the ironic as the result of
illusions and pretensions.

15. *The Tragedy of American Diplomacy,* rev. and enl. ed. (New York: Dell, 1962),
pp. 2–3. For other significant uses of the term tragedy or tragic for which irony or
ironic could be substituted, see *The Tragedy of American Diplomacy,* 1st ed. (Cleveland, World, 1959), pp. 200, 209, and Williams, *The Roots of the Modern American
Empire* (New York: Random House, 1969), p. 46. Subsequent references to this work
appear in the text.

I am indebted to Gary Ostrower for penetrating and helpful comments on the relationship between Williams' concept of tragedy and Niebuhrian irony. I am also indebted to a sensitive and sympathetic review by John Higham of *The Contours of
American History,* in which he notes in a general way Williams' similarity to the
consensus historian in his perception of America "as an essentially homogeneous culture" ("The Contours of William A. Williams," *Studies on the Left,* 2 [1961], 74).

More significant than his use of the term tragic in a sense similar to our use of ironic is the way in which the pattern perceived by Williams in the history of American foreign policy fits the Niebuhrian model. This is particularly evident in *The Roots of the Modern American Empire,* his study of the democratic sources of American imperialism. American farmer-businessmen, a vast part of the population, developed a belief in the overseas expansion of their markets as a cure for the economic ills that beset them late in the nineteenth century. In spite of his own deep agrarian sympathies, Williams is explicit about the responsibility of the farmers for the development of American imperialism. *"I came to see that the expansionist outlook that was entertained and acted upon by metropolitan American leaders during and after the 1890's was actually a crystallization in industrial form of an outlook that had been developed in agricultural terms by the agrarian majority of the country between 1860 and 1893"* (p. xvi; italics in original). Williams emphasizes how broad the responsibility was: "An involvement of the majority of the adult population played a vital part in the evolution and adoption of the imperial policy at the end of the nineteenth century. American imperialism was not forced on the majority by a domestic elite" (p. 5). For Williams the irony of modern American foreign policy is an irony of the American people as a whole.

He sees the drive toward overseas expansion as a symptom of the tendency for Americans to deal with social and economic problems by evading them rather than "by making structural changes in the existing capitalist system" (pp. 16–17). Our frontier experience involved escape from, rather than confrontation with, our social problems. When the frontier was gone it seemed natural to continue in the same pattern by trying to spread our markets throughout the world. "Such an export drive was a major alternative open to the agricultural business, and they rapidly came to stress that solution over all others" (p. 19).

The farmers had ideological as well as economic motives in seeking to expand American markets and influence. Their purpose was not only to preserve and enlarge their own prosperity and freedom but also to increase the prosperity and freedom of others. The definition of the freedom they sought to extend was economic, "an equation that causally linked the free marketplace with freedom per se. The true entrepreneur was a free producer who created plenty for all by operating in a free marketplace" (p. 15). Williams summarizes the motives of American farmers so as to emphasize the interrelatedness of economic and selfless ideological goals.

There have been times when the farmer's export-dominated relationship with the world marketplace led him to develop and advocate a vigorously assertive and expansionist foreign policy, or to support such a policy formulated by others. And, since he actively and causally related his freedom in the marketplace with his personal, political and social freedom, the farmer was strongly inclined to defend and justify such expansionism on the grounds that it extended the freedom of all men. Opening the foreigner's marketplace, he often argued, would open the foreigner's society for the foreigner. American farmers evolved and agitated just such a militantly expansionist foreign policy between 1860 and 1893. That policy played a major causal role in the advent of American imperialism after 1893, and continued to exert a pervasive influence on American thinking about foreign affairs throughout the twentieth century. (p. xxiii)

Williams refers to "the nineteenth-century agricultural majority" as "those men and women [who] embraced imperialism in the name of freedom, as well as in the practice of expanding the marketplace" (p. 452).

The farmers were successful in having their policy of expansion adopted by the nation, but the consequences were not what they had sought. Instead of "the expansion of freedom and the expansion of the marketplace" (p. 450) there was war. "The policy of expanding the free marketplace led unfortunately to wars: wars to apply the principles; and wars to defend the freedom and the prosperity that the expansion of the principles had ostensibly produced for Americans. Finally, after long years, it became clear that the expansion of the free marketplace had failed to bring freedom and prosperity to all Americans, let alone to all the people of the world" (p. 46).

The farmers had a domestic political goal as well as economic and ideological aims in advocating expansion, but the results of that policy were ironic in that respect also. The agricultural majority saw in overseas growth a means of resisting the increasing dominance within the nation of the industrial and commercial minority. They had to expand overseas "not only to win . . . markets, but also in order to realize their majority rights and influence against the power of the American metropolis. The farmers who were quasi-colonials in the domestic economy thus became anticolonial imperialists in foreign affairs as a strategy of becoming equals at home" (p. 25). They were successful in getting the nation to adopt the expansionist policy they advocated, but that success led to a result opposed to the one they sought. "The American colonials who had used expansion to gain a more equitable and profitable relationship with the metropolis became in the process an integral part of an imperial American metropolis'' (pp. 444–45). By converting the nation to expansionism the farmers changed their own character and that of the nation in entirely unintended ways.

Williams is quite explicit about the flaws in the agricultural majority that led them to act so as to bring about results contrary to their wishes. The primary failure of the farmers lay in the narrowness of their conception of freedom. They accepted the basic ideas of Adam Smith and John Locke, which defined freedom in narrowly economic terms. In discussing their attitude toward those who tried to resist American expansion—the specific case is Hawaii—Williams makes it clear that their conception of freedom in general led them to act so as to undermine the realization of their own intentions.

> When freedom was used against the free American marketplace conception of reality, then freedom became unfreedom and intervention was justified as preserving and extending freedom. There was no hypocrisy involved, merely a different estimate of whether freedom would be misused and thereby weaken freedom. The primary limitations on freedom came not from evil or ignorant men, but rather from defining freedom in terms of the marketplace . . . to define freedom as including action removing a vital element from the American marketplace required a different conception of freedom. (p. 436)

In concluding this book, Williams answers affirmatively his rhetorical question, "whether or not the *inherent character* of the marketplace conception of reality sets limits on the nature of freedom" (p. 451). What Americans did was to perceive the rest of the world as if it was an extension of America, and "the result was an overpowering imperial consensus that defined freedom in terms of what existed in America; or, in its most liberal form, in terms of what Americans sought for themselves" (p. 450).[16]

The ironic pattern at the heart of *The Roots of the Modern American Empire* is very clear. American farmers, the majority of the population, sought through overseas expansion to preserve and increase their own wealth and freedom, to hold back the growing power of the metropolitan minority, and to improve the political and economic

---

16. Williams also describes the farmers as suffering from illusions of power. "The great surge in exports also had the important effect of generating a growing certainty about the strength and power of the American economy. That was especially noticeable among the farmers and their spokesmen, who interpreted the boom as proof of their ability to control the markets of the world, as well as convicing evidence of their major role in the American economy" (p. 22). See pages 8, 9, and 43 for comments on the role of illusions of American power and influence as causes of the Mexican and Spanish-American wars.

conditions of foreign peoples, but because of their illusions about the nature of freedom and the universal applicability of American patterns, the policy they advocated led to war and to the transformation of the nation into a commercial and industrial empire, the last thing they had sought. That empire was not the result of the power of the upper class, as some other New Left historians would have it, but rather the democratic if unintended consequence of the pretensions and illusions of the majority of Americans. The responsibility for the failure of basic reform and the evil results of American imperialism belongs not only to an elite but to the American people as a whole.

Since Williams sees escapist and pretentious habits of mind arising out of past experience and becoming major factors in the development and continuation of self-destructive policies, he offers a hope, like that of the ironic historian, that the study of history may be therapeutic. He writes that "history is a way of learning . . . . The historical experience is not one of staying in the present and looking back. Rather it is one of going back into the past and returning to the present with a wider and more intense consciousness of the restrictions of our former outlook. We return with a broader awareness of the alternatives open to us and armed with a sharper perceptiveness with which to make our choices. In this manner it is possible to loosen the dead hand of the past and transform it into a living tool for the present and the future."[17] For Williams it is possible to "transform history as a way of learning into a way of breaking the chains of the past. For by watching other men confront the disparity between existing patterns of thought and a reality to which they are no longer relevant, the outsider may be encouraged to muster his own moral and intellectual courage and discipline and undertake a similar re-examination and re-evaluation of his own outlook" (pp. 479–80). More specifically, Williams argues that in America the study of the past can offer us the self-awareness to overcome "the persistence of a frontier-expansionist outook—a conception of the world and past American history—which holds that expansion . . . offers the best way to resolve problems and to create, or take advantage of, opportunities" (p. 483). That outlook expresses an "urge to escape, to run away" from the problems of establishing "commonwealth" or "community" in America. The creation of such a community, "the first truly democratic socialism in the world," would be "the only real frontier available to Americans in the second half of the 20th century. If they

17. Williams, *The Contours of American History* (Chicago, Quadrangle, 1966), pp. 19–20. Subsequent references to this work appear in the text.

revealed and acted upon the kind of intelligence and morality and courage that it would take to explore and develop that frontier, then they would have finally broken the chains of their own past. Otherwise, they would ultimately fall victims of a nostalgia for their childhood'' (p. 488). Williams recognizes that his hope for a therapeutic history requires the acceptance by the majority of Americans of a share of responsibility for the consequences of American expansionism, because the belief that this policy was merely the result of ruling-class manipulation permits no expectation of a general transformation of consciousness, which would lead to a change in the policy. He implies that such a belief can be an excuse for democratic irresponsibility: ''There was . . . no elite or other scapegoat to blame and replace. There are only ourselves to confront and change. If we can understand how we became an imperial metropolis in the name of the freedom and prosperity of the country, then perhaps we can free our minds and our wills to achieve freedom and prosperity without being an imperial society'' (*Modern American Empire,* p. 46).[18]

History, then, for Williams is a way of liberating ourselves from the past, a way of exposing our democratic tendencies toward escapism so that we can overcome those tendencies in the present. Although this is not expressed precisely in the language of the ironic pattern, it amounts to a very similar conception of the utility of historical knowledge.

Implicit and explicit in Williams' work are beliefs about America and history which are like those of Hartz and are appropriate to an ironic vision. People, for Williams, are complex and contradictory creatures subject to illusions and given to acting so as to produce unintended consequences. These human traits are highly visible in America, where a marketplace mentality and a tendency to escape into expansionism have prevented us from confronting our basic so-

18. In another context Williams implies that what we have to learn from history—and explicitly from Karl Marx—is that we are a part of the human community. On the American continent, ''Nature offered, and Americans seized a way of becoming a world unto themselves'' (*The Great Evasion: An Essay on the Contemporary Relevance of Karl Marx and on the Wisdom of Admitting the Heretic into the Dialogue about America's Future* [Chicago: Quadrangle, 1964], p. 12). See Williams, *Tragedy,* 1st ed., for his use of a quote from Joseph Schumpeter to the effect that ''the American Dream was to become 'a world unto itself.' '' He expresses the hope that historical consciousness can lead us to overcome such a dream, to recognize our limitations, and overcome the tragedy implicit in our history (pp. 19, 20, 209, 210). In this regard Williams is strikingly similar to Hartz, who sees history as a way of overcoming the American tendency to conceive of our fragmented view of the world as if it were the world itself.

cial problems directly and effectively. We have sought to ensure our own wealth and freedom, to spread the benefits of our democracy, and to preserve our agrarian innocence by extending our markets throughout the world, but our expansion has failed to guarantee prosperity for many Americans, has created suffering, hostility, and war abroad, and has contributed to the transformation of America into a metropolitan empire. Over and over Williams emphasizes how our expansionist policies have reflected the values and assumptions of the majority of Americans, not simply those of a dominant elite. For Williams, that majority has acted so as to produce unintended consequences because of its tendency to escape from basic social problems, because of its narrow conception of freedom, and because of its illusion that the American way is best for all nations—ideas that are very similar to Hartz's concept of America as a liberal fragment fleeing from its own roots. Williams argues, as does Hartz, that a historical understanding of our escapist illusions and universalist pretensions can free us to deal more realistically and humanly with our present world. Although his language and the specific historical questions on which he focuses are different and his values more explicit, still a focus on the implicit irony in Williams' work reveals a remarkable resemblance to Hartz.[19]

IV

Gabriel Kolko is one of the most important of the New Left historians in the generation following Williams. In direct contrast to Williams he sees both American internal and foreign policy as the direct products of the intentions of those who possess power in America. (He does concede that in some ways American foreign policy has

19. It is perhaps not too far-fetched to suggest that in a crude way the similarities of ironic form and the differences of historical substance between Hartz's and Williams' work parallel the similarities and differences in the works of Hegel and Marx, both of whom can be read as applying patterns like Niebuhrian irony to history. Certainly there is much evidence to suggest that Hartz's thought is in some sense Hegelian and Williams' is in some sense Marxist. For evidence of irony in Hegel see his *Philosophy of History*, trans. J. Sibree (New York: Dover, 1956), pp. 27, 30, 33, and Walter Kaufman, *Hegel: Reinterpretation, Texts, and Commentary* (Garden City, N. Y.: Doubleday, 1965), p. 174. Marx and Engels are even closer to the Niebuhrian ironic form than is Hegel. See Engels, *Ludwig Feuerbach and the Outcome of Classical German Philosophy* (New York: International Publishers, n.d.), pp. 58–61; Marx, *The Eighteenth Brumaire of Louis Bonaparte* (New York: International Publishers, n.d.), p. 14; Marx and Engels, *Correspondence, 1846–1895* (New York: International Publishers, 1936), pp. 475–77; Eugene Goodhart, *Culture and the Radical Conscience* (Cambridge, Mass.: Harvard Univ. Press, 1973), pp. 105–10; and, for a different perspective on Marxist irony, Hayden White, "Interpretation in History," *New Literary History* 4 (1973), 281–314.

unintended consequences in the outside world, but that concession does not affect his nonironic vision of America and Americans.) Kolko's avoidance of irony differs from Boorstin's not only in the sense that Boorstin has a highly favorable view of America, whereas Kolko is very critical; Boorstin's vision lacks irony primarily because he sees Americans as unreflective pragmatists responding directly to opportunity. In contrast, Kolko's lacks irony because he argues that American leaders have been able to implement the policies they choose without interference. Boorstin sees Americans as having only intentions that are given to their circumstances; Kolko denies the gap between intention and consequence in the domestic history of America. Kolko's American leaders do have intentions that conflict with existing reality, but they are able to shape the country, although not the world, in accordance with those intentions.

Kolko's general account of the Progressive period depends upon a perception of the economic history of the late nineteenth and early twentieth centuries different from that of most other historians. Rather than perceiving it as an age of monopoly, Kolko sees this as a time in which business leaders were deeply disturbed by the disorder and insecurity created by competition. Progressivism on the national level was the result of their deliberate and calculated effort to mobilize the power of the federal government to protect themselves and the capitalist system from the effects of competition. From the beginning of his study Kolko strongly emphasizes the need to examine intentions as well as consequences. He criticizes earlier historians for focusing on the latter to the neglect of the former. "Histories of America from the turn of the century onwards have all too frequently been obsessed by effects rather than causes. Theories and generalizations based upon such an approach have ignored concrete actions and intentions, and for this reason the study of consequences and effects has also been deficient." He examines each of the "progressive" acts "for its intentions and consequences in altering existing power arrangements" and finds that the intentions and results were the same, "to preserve existing power and social relationships."[20]

Insofar as such an account draws the coherence between the motives behind actions and their effects to the center of our attention, it is incompatible with irony. If "political intervention in the economy was frequently merely a response to the demands of particular businessmen"—the men who held power in America—then there is

---

20. Kolko, *The Triumph of Conservatism: A Reinterpretation of American History, 1900–1916* (Glencoe, Ill.: The Free Press, 1963), pp. 1, 2. Subsequent references to this work appear in the text.

no place among such men for the human frailties that lead to ironic behavior. Kolko seems to exclude pretensions and self-deception from his general vision of the ways in which historical events may take place. He is no determinist, but the only alternative to determinism that he seems to see is the effective power of men who know what they want: "The triumph of conservatism that I will describe in detail throughout this book was the result not of any impersonal, mechanistic necessity but of the conscious needs and decisions of specific men and institutions" (p. 2). This statement suggests that history is either the fulfillment of the conscious motives of some people or the result of "mechanistic necessity," ignoring the possibility that much of history may be the unintended outcome of human action, with the discrepancy due primarily to unconscious weaknesses and illusions of the historical actors. Such a conception of the historical process is, of course, profoundly anti-ironical.

Although Kolko sees the national leaders of progressivism—the men prominent in the administrations of Theodore Roosevelt, Taft, and Wilson—as the conscious allies of big business, he acknowledges that there were some Progressives, particularly among those active on a state level, who sincerely sought government regulation in the interest of public good. One of the motives of the business leaders was to deflect the reform energies being mobilized by such people: "It is increasingly obvious that change was inevitable in a political democracy where Grangers, Populists, and trade unionists had significant and disturbing followings and might tap a socially dangerous grievance at some future time and threaten the entire fabric of the status quo, and that the best way to thwart change was to channelize it" (p. 58). The major Progressive leaders—allied with big business—were successful in this. "National progressivism was able to short-circuit state progressivism, to hold nascent radicalism in check by feeding the illusions of its leaders—leaders who could not tell the difference between federal regulation *of* business and federal regulation *for* business" (p. 285). By this account Americans fell exclusively into two categories, the powerful national business and political leaders who ran the country on the one hand, and the local Progressive leaders and their potential mass following, who were duped by the national leaders, on the other. The local leaders were subject to illusions but had no power to affect the course of history; the national leaders were men of power who suffered from no illusions. The members of neither category are seen as fallible human beings with limited control over their destinies.

The appropriation of genuine, local progressivism by the national representatives of the interests of big business is a peripheral story in *The Triumph of Conservatism,* a story told from the point of view of the national rather than that of the local leaders. It would have been compatible with the logic of Kolko's own account to place at the center of the picture the reformers who sincerely sought to limit business in the national interest. If big business felt it necessary to deflect the efforts of those reformers, then the reformers must have been seen as representing, actually or potentially, a large segment of the American people. Kolko's decision to focus on the national rather than the local leaders amounts to a deliberate rejection of an ironic perspective. Utilizing the information that Kolko provides, one could construct an ironic account of progressivism from the point of view of the "genuine" Progressive leaders and the public who supported them as follows. Around the turn of the century, American reformers attempted to assert the power of the federal government against the growing power of the great corporations. The business leaders and their potential allies took hold of this movement and turned it to their own advantage, leading to consequences opposed to those sought by the reformers. The business leaders were able to do this in part because of the illusions of the reformers themselves. But the center of Kolko's attention is too sharply focused on the business leaders, and he is too concerned with their monolithic power, to present such an ironic view even as a minor theme. He explicitly denies that "the extension of federal regulation over the economy" is "a question of progressive intent thwarted by conservative administration and fulfillment. Important business elements could always be found in the forefront of agitation for . . . regulation, and the fact that well-intentioned reformers worked with them—indeed were often indispensable to them—does not change the reality that federal economic regulation was generally designed by the regulated interest to meet its own end, and not those of the public or the commonweal" (p. 59). He repeatedly emphasizes the control of the business interests over progressivism at the national level, from beginning to end. "The basic causal factor behind national progressivism was the needs of business and financial elements" (p. 285). "It was not a coincidence that the results of progressivism were precisely what many major business interests desired. Ultimately businessmen defined the limits of political intervention, and specified its major form and thrust" (p. 280). For such powerful men there could be no discrepancy between their intentions and the consequences of their actions. "The effects of the legislation were only the logical conclusion of the intentions behind it" (p. 283).

Kolko makes essentially the same argument in more cautious detail in regard to one specific industry in his *Railroads and Regulation.* He maintains that "the railroads, not the farmers and shippers, were the most important single advocates of federal regulation."[21] The railroads sought regulation primarily as a means of overcoming the chaotic effects of competition in their industry; they also wanted it "to cope with the unpredictable threat of control by various states . . . . They saw in certain forms of federal regulation of railroads the solution to their many economic problems as well as the redirection of public reform sentiments toward safer outlets" (pp. 4, 5).

As in *The Triumph of Conservatism,* Kolko's focus here is on the industry itself, a focus which he justifies by the neglect of its role by previous historians. Others have concentrated on "the views and actions of politicians, farmers and shippers," but "the role of the railroads and railroad men in the movement for federal regulation has largely been ignored" (p. 6). In rectifying this balance Kolko is drawn away from a perception of unintended consequences—which might characterize the situation of the "farmers and shippers"—and toward the realization of intentions, because in his view the railroads got pretty much what they wanted. Although the evidence he offers in this work for the efforts of the industry to secure federal regulation is more detailed and persuasive than that offered in *The Triumph of Conservatism,* he still makes implicit use of the argument that because the consequences of regulation were favorable to the railroads, they had intended to support regulation from the beginning. The general conclusion that Kolko draws from this study is the same as that which he draws in his broader work on the period, and it has the same implication that there was no discrepancy between intention and consequence in the history of progressivism. "Railroad regulation was the first of many successful efforts to create rationalization and stability in the economy by political means. The goal of these efforts was no progressivism in the traditional sense, as historians have commonly interpreted that term, but a political capitalism which solved the internal problems of an industry and protected it from the attacks of a potentially democratic society" (p. 239). Once again Kolko appears to assume that because federal regulation resulted in "political capitalism" it was intended by those who sought it, thus ignoring the ironic possibility that it was an unintended consequence of ineffectual reform seized by businessmen who themselves only discovered how government regulation could be used in their own interest in the process of struggling over it.

In contrast to his work on domestic history, Kolko's extensive

21. Kolko, *Railroads and Regulation, 1877–1916* (New York: Norton, 1970), p. 3. Subsequent references to this work appear in the text.

writings on American foreign policy contain a pattern similar to the ironic. He sees a tendency for American policy to produce unintended consequences in actions such as involvement in Vietnam, and he actually refers to this as ironic.

> Ironically, instead of accepting the lesson of its failures when its goals exceeded its resources, as in China, the United States' inability to control the Asian revolution led to yet new escalations, temporary successes along with final defeats, and to the ultimate *cul de sac*—Vietnam. Ironic, as well, was the fact that it was this very process of violence, repression, and support to traditional regimes—as in Greece, China, and Vietnam—that made them more self-confidently corrupt and violent, mobilizing and generating their own resistance, polarizing each society yet more deeply, and telescoping the development of national revolutionary movements everywhere.[22]

An unintended effect of American intervention in Vietnam is weakness in other areas of the world: "Ironically, while the United States struggles in Vietnam and the Third World to retain its own mastery, or to continue that once held by former colonial powers, it simultaneously weakens itself in its deepening economic conflict with Europe, revealing the limits of America's power to attain its ambition to define the preconditions and direction of global economic and political developments."[23]

Sometimes Kolko appears to find the reason for American failure in American leaders themselves and their illusions of limitless power. They failed to see that "no nation in this century has had the capacity to control the destiny of more than a very small fraction of the earth's surface" (*Limits of Power,* p. 477). But, in spite of such occasional references to pretensions and self-deceptions on the part of American leaders, the weight of Kolko's interpretation of the reasons why American policy produced unintended consequences lies elsewhere. He emphasizes the hard external fact that "the world had proved too complex and too large for Washington's guidance" (p. 329). In particular, we could not control the third world, where autonomous forces were operating. In his formulation it is as if there is a historical law operating in this. "From the elitist nationalist revolutions to the mass armed peasant uprisings, from the military coup and Putsch to the urban guerrillas, the spontaneous, decentralized nature of change

22. Joyce and Gabriel Kolko, *The Limits of Power: The World and United States Foreign Policy, 1945–1951* (New York: Harper & Row, 1972), p. 714.
23. Kolko, *The Roots of American Foreign Policy: An Analysis of Power and Purpose* (Boston, Beacon, 1969), p. 89.

defied America's control. So long as there is oppression, and exploitation exists, there will be resistance, violence, and conflict" (p. 713). For Kolko the main explanation for the failure of American policy is the resistance of the people of the third world themselves.

Kolko's account of American foreign policy differs from an ironic perspective, and from Williams' account, most clearly in his conception of how that policy is made and in his characterization of those who make it. In Kolko's view national policy directly expresses the interests of the capitalists, a virtual ruling class, who dominate American society and government. "This dominant class, above all else, determines the nature and objectives of power in America. And for this reason no one can regard business as just another interest group in American life, but as the keystone of power which defines the social order, with its security and continuity as an institution being the political order's central goal in the post-Civil War historical experience" (*Roots of Foreign Policy*, p. 9). This class knows and gets what it wants. In Kolko's view of America there are always superpowerful men behind the men who make political decisions, "and should high status, rich men ever seek to make decisions dysfunctional to the more permanent interests of dominant power interests, even more powerful leaders would immediately purge them from decision-making roles" (p. 15). This dominant class does not have significant disagreement within itself. There may be some apparent internal conflict over such issues as the war in Vietnam, but "all the various American leaders believe in global stability, which they are committed to defend against revolution that may threaten the existing distribution of economic power in the world" (p. 15).

Although Kolko draws our attention to the failures and unintended consequences of American policy outside the United States, this conception of the deliberateness and control with which that policy is formed precludes the elements of irony. He emphatically denies "that conflict and violence are accidental rather than inevitable consequences of American foreign policy and the imperatives it has imposed on movements of social transformation throughout the world" (*Limits of Power*, p. 7). Neither accidents, errors, nor faulty visions of reality have shaped American policy.

> That policy and practice have been deliberative and quite consistent because the goals, structure, and requirements of the United States' social system have remained durable throughout the period. The notion of American leadership's errors or misperceptions is reassuring to those who believe the society can be redeemed merely by abler, superior

men. But that species of liberal theory ignores the reasons for the consistency and also the justifications and explanations for action any careful student of the facts will encounter during any judiciously objective search of the historical sources. Official speeches and memoirs are, of course, frequently devoid of revelations of true motives. But articulate men, with a clear sense of purpose and objectives, invariably are at the helm: even their obfuscations often have reasons. (pp. 7–8)

Men of such certain purpose and absolute control may act so as to produce unintended consequences, but when they are presented in this way the source of the discrepancy between their intention and the outcome of their action is found in the world and not in themselves. If one disapproves of their action they may be judged guilty, but they do not suffer from illusions and pretensions, nor does one see virtues linked to their flaws.

Kolko's nonironic view of American history comes closest to Boorstin's in the relative innocence which he, in contrast to Williams, ascribes to the American people. He does not deny that masses of Americans may accept evil policies, but they have no responsibility for such policies. "Mass consent in a society based on a relatively small elite predominance is less significant, and the operative causal agents in society are the interests and goals of men of power—and their ability to retain mastery—rather than masses who also endorse those objectives" (*Roots of Foreign Policy,* p. 12). The opinion of the American people is not responsible for American foreign policy. "Serious students of modern American foreign relations will rarely, if ever, find an instance of an important decision made with any reference to the alleged general public desires or opinions. What is more significant is the fact of ignorance and lack of interest among the vast majority of the population during a period of crisis as to the nature of essential issues and facts, a condition that neutralizes their role in the decision-making process even more and cultivates an elitist attempt for the inchoate role of 'the people' as nothing more than the instrument or objective, rather than the source, of policy" (pp. 13–14). Although Kolko suggests that when public opinion does oppose an action desired by the leaders of America, that opinion may be forcefully repressed rather than simply ignored, the normal relationship between the leadership and the public is manipulative (pp. 88, 89).

Whereas Williams made serious efforts to sort out the complex interaction between mass agrarian opinion and the desires of a commercial elite in the formation of late-nineteenth-century imperialism, Kolko maintains that twentieth-century American policy is simply the direct expression of the goals of that elite with no significant reference to public opinion. Even though this view allows for unintended consequences arising from the intractability of the outside world, it is profoundly incompatible with irony because it is totally without moral ambiguity. The leaders of America are powerful, manipulative, and guilty; the masses are powerless, manipulated, and innocent. Such history may appear to be critical, but for any author or reader who identifies with the people rather than the leadership it is very comforting.

Kolko's vision of America in general is highly incompatible with an ironic sense of the mixture of power and illusion, virtue and evil, in historical actors.[24] He appears to regard Americans as either knaves or fools, dupers or duped. The upper class, which runs the corporations, also runs the country, partly by manipulating the rest of the people, so that always and consistently national policy, both domestic and foreign, expresses its interests and wishes. In his view most Americans are exploited, but unlike the exploited people of the third world they do not have the sense, consciousness, or power to combat their exploitation effectively. In such an America, irony is impossible; those who possess power possess it too absolutely, know their own interest too well, and are too free of inner doubts, conflicts, and illusions to act ironically; the rest of the Americans are too powerless and too unconscious to act at all. Even if America's leaders make us act in ways that produce unintended consequences in our relations with other nations, America itself remains free of irony because by his account the cause of the discrepancy between desire and result lies in the outside world and not in ourselves.

24. An article on Max Weber, published early in Kolko's career, gives some evidence of Kolko's tendency to be insensitive to the historical perception of the disjunction between intentions and consequences. Kolko argues that Weber misunderstood colonial America and that his theory of the relationship between Protestantism and the development of capitalism conflicts with the evidence of colonial history. One claim made by Kolko is that "Nowhere in Weber is there a consideration of the extent to which Calvinist or Puritan doctrine provided a hindrance to continuous rationalized economic behavior and capital accumulation" ("Max Weber on America: Theory and Evidence," *History and Theory,* 1 [1961], 245). He implicitly collapses the unintended consequences of Puritan actions and their conscious intentions here, assuming that since Weber emphasized the contribution that Protestantism made to the development of capitalism he could not have been aware of the tendencies of Puritanism that ran counter to that development. Kolko seems specifically blind to the way in which Weber focuses on the discrepancy between intention and consequences in this, but that is precisely what the great sociologist was talking about: "The cultural consequences of the Reformation were to a great extent, perhaps on the particular aspects with which we are dealing predominantly, unforeseen and even unwished for results of the labours of the reformers. They were often far removed from or even in contradiction to all that they themselves thought to attain" (Weber, *The Protestant Ethic and the Spirit of Capitalism,* trans. Talcott Parsons [New York: Scribner's, 1958] pp. 89–90).

Kolko, like Williams, is a man of the Left, but his vision of America has more in common with that of the conservative Daniel Boorstin. Boorstin's central thesis about what America is—the land of givenness, where the "is" and the "ought" are one—excludes irony by definition. Although Kolko's history is less specifically anti-ironic, in the end it has very similar implications. His focus on the ability of the powerful to control decision-making draws our attention away from the unconscious responsibility of the majority of Americans for what the nation does and away from any possible inner contradictions in the ruling class, away from those traits that lead to ironic action. If Boorstin tends to deny American evil, Kolko identifies that evil exclusively with the ruling class. In the end, for both of them the majority of Americans remain innocent.

V

The works considered in this essay have not been subjected to anything remotely resembling a thorough literary critique. Such a critique would have as its primary purpose a more or less complete exploration and evaluation of these histories as literature. (Since Boorstin clearly writes the best prose among these historians, a purely literary evaluation would lead to conclusions rather different from those of this essay.) I have attempted a simpler and narrower task—to compare these studies to a model of a certain kind of irony. Through that comparison I have tried to show how even such a limited literary analysis can clarify the interpretative and moral significance of historical writing. My literary critique is intended to serve the ends of history by breaking established modes of historiographic perception and exposing connections that were previously obscure.

Examined in terms of irony, Hartz and Williams have much more in common with each other than either has with Boorstin or Kolko. America is understood by Hartz and Williams to be a nation that produces unintended consequences, in part because Americans suffer from illusions and pretensions. Whereas Boorstin may acknowledge some faults in his fundamentally good America, and perhaps Kolko recognizes some virtue in his basically evil one, Hartz and Williams both see an imperfect country in which virtue and evil are characteristically linked. Their conceptions of history are essentially open ended; people can change the direction in which events move, although they cannot bend everything to their will. Hartz and Williams perceive history as an active, human, and temporal process involving intentions, actions, and consequences. For these two historians the function of the study of the past is to liberate people from it, to expose the limitations and distortions in their vision of themselves and the world so that they will be freer to act more realistically and more effectively.

These similarities between Hartz and Williams suggest that historiographers have been too concerned with the overt political views they find in works of history. Boorstin may be an apologist for America, but the example of Hartz shows that not all consensus historians are uncritical. Kolko may have a vision of America as monolithically evil, but Williams is one New Left historian who certainly does not share that vision. Although consensus and New Left history are generally seen as opposed to each other, an ironic analysis leads us to see possible continuities between some historians in each of those categories. Writing in the midst of the cold war, Hartz was able to achieve a remarkable degree of critical detachment, even if he and others like him failed to recognize adequately the social evils of America, the evils of racism, sexism, poverty, and "democratic imperialism." These, of course, are the major concerns of many New Left historians. This difference has been seen as evidence of the repudiation by the younger historians of their predecessors, but if we shift our angle of vision perhaps it might be possible to see in some New Left history a further development, rather than a repudiation, of some consensus history. A New Left historian like Williams offers a much more explicitly critical vision of the American past than that presented by Hartz, but that vision can be seen as a further development and maturation of aspects of its predecessors' work. Literary analysis may not be the only way to expose this continuity, but it is one effective way. An important link between consensus and New Left history is the literary form of Niebuhrian irony, which draws our attention at once to the virtues and evils in America, to the connection between them, and to the unconscious responsibility of Americans for that evil.[25] In general I suspect that other studies of this kind,

25. Niebuhrian irony can be found in the writings of many historians of America, although obviously by no means in all of them. Gene Wise and Henry May have discussed Perry Miller's use of the form (Wise, *American Historical Explanations* and "Implicit Irony," and May, "Perry Miller's Parrington," *American Scholar,* 25 (1966), 562–70. Among earlier historians it is particularly evident in the work of Henry Adams and Carl Becker, although, surprisingly, V. L. Parrington also uses Niebuhrian irony in the last volume of *Main Currents in American Thought.* In addition to Hartz, among consensus historians, Richard Hofstadter's *American Political Tradition* is largely shaped by irony and it also informs the work of Alexander L. and Juliette L. George, R. W. B. Lewis, Marvin Meyer, David Noble, Charles Sanford, Henry Nash Smith, William R. Taylor, and John William Ward. Among New Left historians it is particu-

focusing on irony, other structural patterns, styles, or rhetorical modes, may show us other unexpected resemblances among historians that cut across apparent lines of division. In this way the critical methods of literature can serve the ends of historiography.

---

larly evident in the writings of Christopher Lasch, Stephen Thernstrom, and Sam Bass Warner, in addition to Williams. John Rosenberg has explicitly applied a radical version of Niebuhrian irony to the Civil War in "Toward a New Civil War Revisionism," *American Scholar,* 38 (1969), 250–72. One result of New Left social concerns has been a growth of interest in the history of the social life of people of the past in general. Some of these new social historians have no particular connection with the New Left, but many of them make use of Niebuhrian irony. I have found it in the work of Phillip Greven, Jr.; Michael Katz; Kenneth Lockridge; Darrett Rutman; and Richard Sennett. In addition it is used by a number of historians of the South, particularly Steven A. Channing, William Freehling, Winthrop Jordan, and C. Vann Woodward, and by literary historians such as Sacvan Bercovitch.

Louis O. Mink

5
NARRATIVE FORM
AS A COGNITIVE
INSTRUMENT

> One hears about life, all the time, from different
> people, with very different narrative gifts.
> Anthony Powell, *Temporary Kings*

Philosophy does begin with wonder, as Aristotle said, but in popular culture this is usually misunderstood as meaning that the occasions for philosophical speculation are miracles and mysteries, the apparently inexplicable intrusions on quotidian experience. On the contrary, nothing is more wonderful than common sense. The comfortable certainties of what "everybody knows" have been since Socrates a more natural field for philosophical reflection than eclipses, prophecies, monstrosities, and the irruption of unintelligible forces. The common sense of an age, we recognize when we compare that age with others, may well be for different times or places beyond the limits of comprehension or even of fantasy. A primary reason for this is that common sense of whatever age has presuppositions which derive not from universal human experience but from a shared conceptual framework, which determines what shall count as experience for its communicants. For experience centered on one conceptual framework, there are literally sermons in stones or vengeance in the thunderbolt. But for other experience these pereeptions seem poetic fancies, and for yet other experience they are simply unintelligible.

The distinction between history and fiction is as universally shared an item in "common sense" as any distinction in Western culture, at least since the rise of popular literacy. "Everyone knows," as certainly as everyone knows that two bodies cannot occupy the same space at the same time, that history claims to be a true representation of the past while fiction does not, even when it purports to describe actions and events locatable in particular times and places. At the most, fiction demands a temporary suspension of disbelief. Everyone knows that what makes a story good is different from what, if anything, makes it true. Fiction may indeed be accurate in reporting some events, actions, and the details of life in a certain period, but we know this (and know that we know it), only because we can compare fiction with history, without doubting in principle which is which. Many of the details of life in the fictional Dublin of June 16, 1904, in Joyce's *Ulysses* are also details of the historical Dublin. A horse named Throwaway did win the Gold Cup, and the newspapers did report the *General Slocum* disaster in America. Yet while no work of history captures as well as *Ulysses* the feel of some Dublin life on that day or in that time, we know perfectly well that there are true stories about the careers of Throwaway and of the Dublin newspapers which happen to intersect with *Ulysses,* while there is no such true story about Leopold Bloom. Whether or not he had breakfast in bed on the morning of June 17 is not a historical question, although, as a problem for literary critics, it is crucial to one's interpretation of the fiction.

Histories are of course full of things that are not so, just as fiction is full of things that are so. But this can be said only because for shared common sense there is no problem *in principle* about the distinction between history and fiction. To say that something in a history "isn't so" is to say that it did not happen or was not that way. This acknowledges what history and fiction have in common as well as how they differ. Both the similarity and the difference are, for common sense, clear and uncomplicated. History and fiction are alike stories or narratives of events and actions. But for history both the structure of the narrative and its details are representations of past actuality; and the claim to be a true representation is understood by both writer and reader. For fiction, there is no claim to be a true representation in any particular respect. Even though much might be true in the relevant sense, nothing in the fictional narrative marks out the difference between the true and the imaginary; and this is a convention that amounts to a contract to which writer and reader subscribe. In the absence of this contract we should not be able to play the enchanting games with the verisimilitude of fiction that depend on pretending that the contract does not exist although we know that it does—as in the recreations of the Baker Street Irregulars, which have made Sherlock Holmes a more vividly "historical" figure than Gladstone.

These observations are so far elementary, but even so historians might object. The difference between history and fiction, they might well say, is less a matter of truth than of evidence. One may well disclaim any privileged access to "truth" except as truth-claims are reformulated in terms of the assessment of evidence, a process which historians know well makes all claims inferential and tentative. Of course it is salutary to be reminded that historiography is a matter of fallible inference and interpretation, but the reminder does not touch the point of the common-sense distinction between history and fiction. For that distinction, it is still a matter of what "everyone knows" that the events and actions of past actuality happened *just as they did,* and there is therefore something for historiography, however fallible, to be about, something which makes it true or false even though we have no access to that something except through historical reconstruction from present evidence. The determinateness of the past is part of common-sense ontology; it is not a theory but a presupposition of unreflective common experience. Historians might object, too, to the emphasis on narrative historiography. Professional history, a historian might say, is largely "analytic"; it does not exclude the construction of narrative accounts, but that is a literary art quite independent of professional skill in actual research. Now this objection would be telling if historiography were *defined* as narrative exposition. But the common-sense distinction between history and fiction does not depend on such a tendentious definition. It only acknowledges that a great deal of historiography has been and continues to be narrative in form. Even histories that are synchronic studies of the culture of an epoch inevitably take into account the larger process of development or change in which that epoch was a stage. Huizinga's *The Waning of the Middle Ages,* for example, or Peter Laslett's *The World We Have Lost,* neither of which has a narrative structure, nevertheless indicate even in their titles the narrative relevance of their cross-sectional accounts. The most "analytic" historical monograph, one might say and could show, presupposes the historian's more general understanding, narrative in form, of patterns of historical change, and is a contribution to the correction or elaboration of that narrative understanding. That is what phrases like "pre-industrial society" and "decline and fall" express to our narrative imagination.

Historians would in fact be ill-advised to relegate skill in managing narrative complexity to the status of a merely literary grace irrelevant to the hard cognitive stuff of historical research. Even though narrative form may be, for most people, associated with fairy tales, myths, and the entertainments of the novel, it remains true that narrative is a primary cognitive instrument—an instrument rivaled, in fact, only by theory and by metaphor as irreducible ways of making the flux of experience comprehensible. Narrative form as it is exhibited in both history and fiction is particularly important as a rival to theoretical explanation or understanding. Theory makes possible the explanation of an occurrence only by describing it in such a way that the description is logically related to a systematic set of generalizations or laws. One understands the operation of a spring-powered watch, for example, only insofar as one understands the principles of mechanics, and this requires describing the mechanism of the watch in terms, and *only* in terms, appropriate to those principles. One could not, so to speak, understand the operation of a watch but fail to understand the operation of a mill wheel, or vice versa, unless one had given the wrong description of one or both. But a particular watch also has a historical career: it is produced, shipped, stored, displayed, purchased, used; it may be given and received, lost and found, pawned and redeemed, admired and cursed, responsible for a timely arrival or a missed appointment. At each moment of its career, that is, it is or may be a part of a connected series of events which intersects its own history, and at each such moment it may be subject to a particular description, which is appropriate only because of that intersection. Now from the standpoint of theoretical understanding, the type of appropriate description is a given; it is not problematic. But the particular *history* of the watch escapes theoretical understanding simply because to envision that history requires the attribution of indefinitely many descriptions of it as they are successively relevant or irrelevant to the sequences that intersect its career. This is what narrative form uniquely represents, and why we require it as an irreducible form of understanding. On the one hand, there are all the occurrences of the world—at least all that we may directly experience or inferentially know about—in their concrete particularity. On the other is an ideally theoretical understanding of those occurrences that would treat each as nothing other than a replicable instance of a systematically interconnected set of generalizations. But between these extremes, narrative is the form in which we make comprehensible the many successive interrelationships that are comprised by a career. Both historians and writers of imaginative fiction know well the problems of constructing a coherent narrative account, with or without the constraint of arguing from evidence, but even so they may not recognize the extent to which narrative as such is not just a technical problem for writers and critics but a primary and irreducible form of human comprehension, an article in the constitution of common sense.

I

Particular narratives express their own conceptual presuppositions. They are in fact our most useful evidence for coming to understand conceptual presuppositions quite different from our own. It is, for example, through the plots of Greek tragedy that we can best understand an idea of Fate that was never explicitly formulated as a philosophical theory and that is far removed from our own presuppositions about causality, responsibility, and the natural order. But while the structure of stories bodies forth a particular conceptual scheme necessary to any understanding of the story, there are also at a more general level conceptual presuppositions of the very idea of narrative form itself, and these supervene on its many varieties. Aristotle's comment that every story has a beginning, a middle, and an end is not merely a truism. It commands universal assent while failing to tell us anything new, simply because it makes explicit part of the conceptual framework underlying the capacity to tell and hear stories of any sort. And in making a presupposition explicit it has implications that are far from banal; it makes clear that our experience of life does not itself necessarily have the form of narrative, except as we give it that form by making it the subject of stories. That this implication is surprising should not be surprising. It merely reflects the difference between the deliverances of common sense and its presuppositions. The former are the comfortable certainties that we know; the latter, though sine qua non's, yield themselves up only to reflection, which finds them wonderful as their implications come to light.

Until recently, the concept of narrative form seemed straightforward and unproblematic (as everything does to common sense). After all, although *kinds* of stories vary widely and significantly from culture to culture, story-telling is the most ubiquitous of human activities, and in any culture it is the form of complex discourse that is earliest accessible to children and by which they are largely acculturated. *How* we understand a story has never seemed a problem. But in recent years the concept of narrative has been increasingly subjected to sophisticated analysis, and with less than satisfactory results. In the critical philosophy of history, narrative has increasingly come to be regarded as a type of explanation different from and displacing scientific or "covering-law" explanation of actions and events. But one result has been the emergence of problems not even recognized before. There is, for example, the problem of explicating how a narrative structure determines what is or is not relevant to it; this problem has no analogue in the explication of the structure of theories. We ordinarily recognize, and in certain clear cases with no uncertainty at all, whether in the recounting of a coherent narrative a specific incident or detail is relevant or irrelevant to *that* narrative. (If I am telling the story of an encounter and its outcome that took place last Wednesday, I might become preoccupied with the incidental fact that it occurred on Wednesday and begin to add other details of what otherwise happened to me on Wednesday, for no better reason than that.) Since we do recognize that a given incident is relevant or irrelevant to a certain narrative, it would seem that we must be in possession of implicit *criteria* of relevance. Just as logic makes explicit the criteria of valid inference, which are implicit in the unreflective recognition of arguments in ordinary discourse as good or bad, so it would seem that we should be able to make explicit in a systematic way the criteria implicit in our recognition of relevance and irrelevance. Yet in fact no one has been able to state in general form any criterion of narrative relevance other than that of causal connection with events already established in the narrative, and not even this is adequate as a criterion. Not all of the causes or effects of an occurrence will be relevant to the story of which it is a part, and therefore an additional criterion is necessary to distinguish those that are from those that are not—and this criterion cannot be that of causal connection. In general, we know that there are many different ways in which an incident may be relevant to a story, but are unable to list the kinds of relevance. Yet one could not accept the alternative that every part of every story is relevant in its own unique way—that is, that there are no *kinds* of relevance.

One conceptual problem about narrative, therefore, is to make explicit the criteria by which in fact we recognize a narrative as coherent or incoherent. But this is a problem for narrative form in general, whether it purports to be history or fiction. I mention it, although I have no criteria of relevance to propose for examination, to illustrate the idea of conceptual problems about narrative as such. There are other problems, more amenable to a solution even though a radical one, which arise, I believe, for the following reason. Just as one conceptual presupposition of common sense has been that historiography consists of narratives which claim to be true, while fiction consists of imaginative narratives for which belief and therefore truth-claims are suspended, so another presupposition has been that historical actuality itself has narrative form, which the historian does not invent but discovers, or attempts to discover. History-as-it-was-lived, that is, is an untold story. The historian's job is to discover that untold story, or part of it, and to retell it even though in abridged or edited form. It is because of this presupposition that historians have not been inclined to value literary skill, or to find instructive the comparison of the historian with the novelist. The presupposition gives the force of self-evidence to the difference between history and fiction. The novelist can make up his story any way he wishes, subject only to the requirements of art. The historian, on the other hand, finds the story already hidden in what his data are evidence for; he is creative in the invention of research techniques to expose it, not in the art of narrative construction. Properly understood, the story of the past needs only to be communicated, not constructed.

But that past actuality is an untold story is a presupposition, not a proposition which is often consciously asserted or argued. I do not know a single historian, or indeed anyone, who would subscribe to it as a consciously held belief; yet if I am right, it is implicitly presupposed as widely as it would be explicitly rejected. (The situation is as it were a mirror image of the explicit belief that the *future* is an untold story, held by those whose controlling presuppositions in all other areas of belief and action are logically incompatible with that belief.) And it is the conflict between implicit presupposition and explicit belief which generates characteristic conceptual problems about the form of narratives to each other. It is these problems—three of them—which it is my main purpose to discuss. But to understand a conceptual problem is to see how it has come to arise. Logically, the source of these problems is the dissonance between implicit presupposition and explicit belief which has been noted. Historically, they are the legacy of the idea that once was called Universal History—an ideal that never became an achievement, but one that served as a regulative principle of thought about the past. The reports of its death have been premature. Although it has disappeared from the discourse of ideas—that is, although it no longer belongs to the structure of conscious belief and controversy—it has, I believe, survived as the presupposition that past actuality is an untold story; and how this came about may be briefly sketched.

II

The idea of Universal History is at least as old as Augustine's *City of God,* and was introduced to modern thought in Vico's *Scienza nuova.* But it was never so powerful or so widely shared as at the end of its active life, the last two decades of the eighteenth century. One of the dramatic moments in its late career was Schiller's inaugural lecture at Jena in May 1789, "Was heisst und zu welchem Ende studiert man Universalgeschichte?" [What is universal history and why do we study it?]. The event was notable, for Schiller was already the idol of the rising generation. The universal historian, he told the cheering members of his audience who had borne him on their shoulders to the lecture hall, explains the whole contemporary world by discerning those chains of events that have led up to the present, and displaying them as a single and coherent whole. Thus it is Universal History, he went on, which alone enables one to understand how stable and enduring peace has been achieved in Europe. The irony of having expressed such a complacent view less than two months before the beginning of Europe's greatest revolution apparently was not borne in upon Schiller even later; in his correspondence during the succeeding years there is not a mention of the world-historical events transpiring only a few hundred miles away. But prophecy was in any case not the point or purpose of Universal History, and if one discerned the grand design of history even a surprising future could be incorporated in it as local detail. Condorcet's optimism about progress as the grand design remained unqualified when he wrote another classical contribution to the theory of Universal History while in prison in 1793 awaiting execution as one of history's victims.

Schiller's inaugural lecture came only five years after Kant's "Idee zu einer allgemeinen Geschichte in weltbürgerliche Absicht" [Idea for a Universal History on a Cosmopolitan Plan] (1784), and shows its influence. Kant, as usual, came close to the heart of the idea. We cannot make sense of history, he says (and he means by history *res gestae,* including the whole record of human folly, vanity, and cruelty) unless it is possible to discover in it a single theme, a "regular movement," so that "what seems complex and chaotic in the single individual may be seen from the standpoint of the human race as a whole to be a steady and progressive though slow evolution of its original endowment." What Kant concluded, of course, is that the plotline of history is the hidden intention of nature that men should, by the use of reason and out of necessity, develop institutions to protect themselves against the otherwise lethal consequences of their own "unsocial sociability"—the combination of selfishness with the need for others. But it is Kant's question rather than his answer that reveals the force of the idea of Universal History. Beyond the level of mere chronologies, can there be anything like historical understanding unless those chronologies can be related to each other in the light of some larger theme about the movement and direction of history?

Universal History was not the idea that there is a particular plot in the movement of history but the assumption that underlay all proposals to display one sort of plot or another. Despite its variations, however, one can analyze certain common features of this complex idea. First, it was the claim that the ensemble of human events belongs to a single story. Yet there is no implication about who devises or tells this story. In its original theological form, as with Augustine, Universal History was the work of divine Providence; but as the idea became secularized by the eighteenth century, God the Author retreated, leaving the idea of a story which is simply *there,* devised by no one (as for Kant the "hidden intention of nature" was a regulative idea, that is, a hypothesis which enables one to ask the right questions but which should be regarded as heuristic rather than as true) but waiting to be told by someone. Nevertheless, the story does include the future, in outline if not in detail. Future events cannot falsify the idea of Universal History, which provides a way of interpreting them so that they will fit its plot. Kant was confident that the denouement of political history would turn out to be a federation of nations, but he was prepared for any amount or kind of national conflict as the terror which would ultimately force men to adopt this rational institution.

Second, the idea of Universal History specifies that there is a single central subject or theme in the unfolding of the plot of history. This aspect of the idea achieved maximum unity and complexity simultaneously with Hegel. It may seem that "central subject or theme" merely makes explicit part of the meaning of "plot"; actually it adds something to the latter notion by making clear that it does not imply that there is a *law* of historical development or that the detailed course of events is inexorable. The idea of Universal History is independent of the question whether there can be a theoretical science of history. Orthodox post-Marxist historical materialism is the main instance of the idea of Universal History surviving into the present century, but it added the postulate of determinism to the idea of Universal History rather than finding that postulate already implied in the idea.

Third, it *is* implied that the events of the historical process are unintelligible when seen only in relation to their immediate circumstances. True, there are local stories, but like individual events their beginnings and ends are arbitrary, and their narrative form not fully determinate, until they are ensconced within the single envisioned story. If it is true that the history of the world would have been different had Cleopatra's nose been half an inch longer, then it follows that the significance of all subsequent stories depends in part on seeing their narrative relationship to expanding circles of plots within plots, until Antony's passion and downfall are reached as a crucial junction of Roman history. This is not as absurd as it may seem. We do in fact acquire and carry with us in imagination some sketchy outline of historical development over long periods, just as we acquire and carry with us imaginative sketches of geography, and in both cases we know that the vast areas of vagueness can if necessary be filled in with detail. Moving about in our immediate environments, we are still peripherally aware as a necessary part of our spatial orientation that Havana is a long way in *that* direction and Tokyo is a good deal longer way in *that* direction. Similarly we know that Rome rose and fell, leaving remains and legacies, and that its history was intertwined with the abilities, ambitions, and passions of individuals. So there are *routes* from events in the past to events in the present. As Universal History was conceived by its proponents, it is not the aggregate of all those routes but rather the grid on which any of them might be traced; and in this sense it is not easy to conceive an alternative to it.

Finally, Universal History did not deny the great diversity of human events, customs, and institutions; but it did regard this variety as the permutations of a single and unchanging set of human capacities and possibilities, differentiated only by the effects of geography, climate, race, and other natural contingencies. Hume's well-known statement expresses this confidence. "It is universally acknowledged," according to Hume, "that there is a great uniformity among the actions of men, in all nations and ages, and that human nature remains still the same, in its principles and operations . . . . Would you know the sentiments, inclinations, and course of life of the Greeks and Romans? Study well the temper and *actions* of the French and English: You cannot be mistaken in transferring to the former *most* of the observations which you have made with regard to the latter. Mankind are so much the same, in all times and places, that history informs us of nothing new or strange in this particular" (*Enquiry Concerning Human Understanding*, VIII, I).

No doubt it was this dependence on the principle of the uniformity of human nature that accounts more than anything else for the decline of the idea of Universal History with the rise of the modern sociological consciousness—that is, with the acceptance of cultural pluralism by modern common sense. But even at the point of its flowering, what the idea of Universal History never made room for was the uniqueness, vividness, and intrinsic value of individuals, whether of individual persons, individual cultures, or individual epochs. My point is not that Universal History was based on an error, which now stands revealed. The incomparability of individuals may well be illusory, but from the standpoint of Universal History the question cannot even arise: it is ruled out by all the features of Universal History just reviewed. If the ensemble of human events belongs to a single story with a central theme or subject, then the lives and deaths of empires as well as of individual men find their significance only in an interpretation that could not in principle be accessible *to them* in their time. All historical agents would be like Rosencrantz and Guildenstern, supporting players who are not around for the denouement. The remarkable thing is that this conclusion, though it now seems inescapable, was never clearly drawn even by Hegel. But it does seem in retrospect as if what we now call Romanticism had discerned and rejected this implication. It brought about—in large part, it *was*— an upsurge of a new historical consciousness which usurped the idea of Universal History. Among the expressions of the Romantic historical consciousness were the neo-Gothic revival and renewed interest in the Middle Ages generally; a new value placed upon folk culture, and the revival and even imitation of folk literature, folk music, folk costume, and folk crafts; at the other extreme of the social and political order, a fascination with the lives of great men and heroes; and the rewriting of national histories to push back to the edges of prehistory the national differences of peoples.

The rise of nationalist history and of history as propaganda for nationalism is the most obvious sign of the dissolution of Universal History, but it seems that most of the features of the Romantic syndrome contributed to its dismantling. Folk traditions, for example, when valued for their own sake, present a spectacle of infinite variety and vivid differences. They are intelligible not as the vehicles of a single story of human development, but as the survivals of many different local stories of continuity and change—stories which over most of their duration have no relevance to each other, as the lives of the peoples in the Scandinavian forests had no points of living contact with the lives of the inhabitants of the Swiss mountain valleys. What all these new interests have in common is the impossibility of being gathered together under any rubric of "universal history." One simply cannot generalize over cultural histories as easily as one can over political history. The history of mankind thus became dispersed into an encyclopedia of biographies, customs, ideas, local institutions, languages, peoples, and nations. The dispersal was summed up in Carlyle's dictum that history is "the essence of innumerable biographies." I first heard this phrase a generation ago from a somewhat disillusioned graduate student in history who thought he had invented it himself; and he probably had. It is a measure of what has happened to the idea of Universal History that such historical nominalism has become just part of shared common sense.

The idea of Universal History of course did not disappear with its name in the Romantic dissolution. It survived through the nineteenth century in the guise of the doctrine of progress, and to the present in the form of orthodox historical materialism. But the view of historical knowledge most widely shared in our time is precisely the denial of the claims of universal history. Instead of the belief that there is a single story embracing the ensemble of human events, we believe that there are many stories, not only different stories about different events, but even different stories about the same events. As Hayden White has persuasively argued in *Metahistory* and in his essay in this volume, the bare chronicle of the historical record can be "emplotted" in different ways (as romance, comedy, tragedy, or satire), which themselves rest not upon arguments from the evidence but upon irreducible imaginative preferences or choices. *A fortiori,* we believe that there are many central subjects or themes for the many stories, and that the differences among them are inadjudicable. Moreover, the many stories have their own beginnings, middles, and ends, and are at least in principle fully intelligible without ensconcing them within a more comprehensive narrative whose form is not fully visible in the segment that they represent. We do believe, it can be said, that historical narratives can be *added* to others, as in the periodization of political history by reigns, or of social history by decades; but this is a convenience made possible by chronology, not by an antecedent understanding of the relation of subplot to main plot. And finally, in the age of anthropology, few can believe in an unchanging and universal human nature whose principles can be learned from any local experience and then confidently applied to the interpretation of all ages and cultures. On the contrary, it has become a rule of historical inquiry that the significance of past actions must in the first instance be understood in terms of their agents' own beliefs, including their beliefs about human nature, not in terms of our possibly very different ones; we must at least understand their own action-descriptions before we venture our own redescriptions.

It seems, therefore, that the idea of Universal History has been discarded upon the midden of the past, along with such refuse as the legitimacy of kings and the perfectibility of man. Yet I venture to claim that the concept of universal *history* has not been abandoned at all, only the concept of universal *historiography*. It makes no more sense to laymen than to professional historians to suppose that a single unified story of the human past could even ideally be written and read. Yet the idea that the past itself is an untold story has retreated from the arena of conscious belief and controversy to habituate itself as a presupposition in that area of our a priori conceptual framework which resists explicit statement and examination. To say that we still presuppose, as a priori, a concept of universal history, means: we assume that everything that has happened belongs to a single and determinate realm of unchanging actuality. ("What's done is done. You can't change the past.") In his *Analytical Philosophy of History,* Arthur Danto imagines an Ideal Chronicler, who would be omniscient about everything occurring contemporaneously with his own experience and who would record accurate descriptions of every event as it occurred. His record would therefore be an Ideal Chronicle, a cumulative account of "what really happened." Danto's strategy in this speculation was to point out that even such an Ideal Chronicle could not supplant historiography by making the latter unnecessary, because it logically could not include a class of characteristically historical statements, namely those that *describe* an event in terms that refer to subsequent events; for example, "On December 28, 1856, the twenty-eighth President of the United States was born." But I refer to the Ideal Chronicle for a different purpose—to point out, merely, that we *understand* the idea of it perfectly clearly. And we could not conceive or imagine an Ideal Chronicle at all *unless* we already had the concept of a totality of "what really happened." We reject the possibility of a historiographical representation of this totality, but the very rejection presupposes the concept of the totality itself. It is in that presupposition that the idea of Universal History lives on.

III

As we know most clearly from the history of science, the most difficult and interesting conceptual problems arise when one theory is replaced by another although the presuppositions (or "metaphysics," or "paradigm") of the former theory persist, unconsciously as it were. The dissonance between new ideas and old presuppositions characteristically produces conceptual confusion and felt discomfort, which only gradually can be brought to formulation as conceptual or epistemological problems. It is always a problem to identify the area of dissonance which might reward rather than resist efforts at analysis. My central thesis is that the questions we should ask are about narrative *form* as a cognitive instrument. It may not seem that this is problematic at all. After all, we commonly and often successfully undertake to explain something by telling the story of how it came to be that way; in this respect a fictional narrative may be as explanatory as a historical narrative although in the one case it is an imaginary event and in the other an actual (or evidenced) event which is explained. Just because such narrative understanding is so common and apparently transparent, my strategy is to create perplexity about the concept of narrative, to make some ambiguities of the concept a discomfort which can be felt.

The first problem arises if we ask how narratives can be related to each other: can two narratives be combined (under suitable restrictions on chronology and coincidence of characters and events) to form a single more complex narrative? In narrative fiction, we ordinarily regard it as possible but not necessary for two or more self-contained narratives to aggregate into a complex whole. Even though *Oedipus Rex* and *Antigone* are plays in the same trilogy, we do at any reasonable level of sophistication regard them as individual works of imagination, and therefore do not count it as a failure on Sophocles' part that the conventional and sagacious Creon of *Oedipus Rex* is not intelligibly continuous with the willful and even blasphemous Creon of *Antigone*. When individual narrative fictions do aggregate, as in Faulkner's record of Yoknapatawpha County or in Trollope's Barsetshire novels, we most naturally construe it as the borrowing, for imaginative and artistic purposes, of the conventions of historical representation. For historical narratives *should* aggregate; insofar as they make truth-claims about a selected segment of past actuality, they must be compatible with and complement other narratives which overlap or are continuous with them. Even if there are different ways of emplotting the same chronicle of events, it remains true that historical narratives are capable of *displacing* each other. This happens, for example, when a narrative makes sense of a series of actions by showing them to be decisions reflecting a consistently held policy, where received accounts could only describe them as arbitrary and surprising reactions, or as irrational responses. But narrative fictions, though they may be more or less coherent, do not displace each other; each, so to speak, creates the unique space which it alone occupies rather than competing with others for the same space as historical narratives may.

Yet while historical narratives ought to aggregate into more comprehensive narratives, or give way to rival narratives which will so aggregate, in fact they do not; and here is where conceptual discomfort should set in. The traditional way of avoiding it, and very analgesic it has been, too, is to distinguish between "objectivity" and "subjectivity." Narrative histories *would* combine into more comprehensive wholes to the extent that they achieve complete objectivity; unfortunately, however, historians have been prone to introduce their individual idiosyncrasies and values both in the selection and in the combination of facts. It is because of the differences in these subjective elements that one historian's narrative does not comport with another's. My purpose is not to decide whether historical objectivity is possible; it is rather to point out that the claim that it is clearly presupposes what I have called the idea of Universal History—that past actuality is an untold story and that there is a right way to tell it even though only in part.

But while objectivity is conceivable for a cumulative *chronicle,* it cannot really be translated into terms of narrative history (and in general the belief in historical objectivity fails to distinguish between narrative and chronicle, which has no form other than that of chronology and no relations among events other than temporal relations.) A narrative must have a unity of its own; this is what is acknowledged in saying that it must have a beginning, middle, and an end. And the reason why two narratives cannot be merely additively combined—in the simplest case, by making them temporally continuous as the parallel chronicle is continuous—is that in the earlier narrative of such an aggregate the end is no longer an end, and therefore the beginning is no longer *that* beginning, nor the middle *that* middle. The more comprehensive narrative may be given its own formal unity, but this is a new unity, which replaces the independent coherence of each of its parts rather than uniting them. Sophocles' trilogy is not itself a play; if it were, its constituents would be not plays but acts.

The point we have reached, therefore, is that narrative histories should be aggregative, insofar as they are histories, but cannot be, insofar as they are narratives. Narrative history borrows from fictional narrative the convention by which a story generates its own imaginative space, within which it neither depends on nor can displace other stories; but it presupposes that past actuality is a single and determinate realm, a presupposition which, once it is made explicit, is at odds with the incomparability of imaginative stories.

Inseparable from the question of how narratives aggregate is a second problem about the sense in which a narrative may be true or false. This question arises only if a narrative as such does have holistic properties, that is, if the *form* of the narrative, as well as its individual statements of fact, is taken as representing something that may be true or false. One can regard any text in direct discourse as a logical conjunction of assertions. The truth-value of the text is then simply a logical function of the truth or falsity of the individual assertions taken separately: the conjunction is true if and only if each of the individual propositions is true. Narrative has in fact been analyzed, especially by philosophers intent on comparing the form of narrative with the form of theories, as if it were nothing but a logical conjunction of past-referring statements; and on such an analysis there is no problem of *narrative truth*. The difficulty with the model of logical conjunction, however, is that it is not a model of narrative form at all. It is rather a model of *chronicle*. Logical conjunction serves well enough as a representation of the only ordering relation of chronicles, which is " . . . and then . . . and then . . . and then . . . " Narratives, however, contain indefinitely many ordering relations, and indefinitely many ways of *combining* these relations. It is such combination that we mean when we speak of the coherence of a narrative, or lack of it. It is an unsolved task of literary theory to classify the ordering relations of narrative form; but whatever the classification, it should be clear that a historical narrative claims truth not merely for each of its individual statements taken distributively, but for the complex form of the narrative itself. Only by virtue of such form can there be a story of failure or of success, of plans miscarried or policies overtaken by events, of survivals and transformations which interweave with each other in the circumstances of individual lives and the development of institutions. But narrative form, to paraphrase what Wittgenstein said of the logical form of a proposition, cannot be "said" but must be "shown"—in the narrative as a whole. We recognize that a narrative cannot be summarized, or restated as an inventory of conclusions or "findings"; not that conclusions may not be drawn, but if one asks for reasons for accepting or rejecting them, the answer is not simply a recital of pieces of evidence (of the sort that would be advanced to support a generalization), but rather the repetition of the way in which the narrative has ordered the evidence. The situation is not unlike the apocryphal story told of many composers, for instance of Schubert: when asked what a sonata he had just played "meant," he responded only by sitting down and playing it again. The difference, of course, is that a historical narrative claims to be true, in a way that music does not.

The cognitive function of narrative form, then, is not just to relate a succession of events but to body forth an ensemble of interrelationships of many different kinds as a single whole. In fictional narrative the coherence of such complex forms affords aesthetic or emotional satisfaction; in historical narrative it additionally claims truth. But this is where the problem arises. The analysis and criticism of historical evidence can in principle resolve disputes about matters of fact or about the relations among facts, but not about the possible combinations of kinds of relations. The same event, under the same description or different descriptions, may belong to different stories, and its particular significance will vary with its place in these different—often very different—narratives. But just as "evidence" does not dictate which story is to be constructed, so it does not bear on the preference of one story to another. When it comes to the narrative treatment of an ensemble of interrelationships, we credit the imagination or the sensibility or the insight of the individual historian. This must be so, since there are no *rules* for the construction of a narrative as there are for the analysis and interpretation of evidence, and historians have acknowledged this in making no attempt whatever to teach the construction of narrative as part of the professional apprenticeship of the historical guild.

So narrative form in history, as in fiction, is an artifice, the product of individual imagination. Yet at the same time it is accepted as claiming truth—that is, as representing a real ensemble of interrelationships in past actuality. Nor can we say that narrative form is like a hypothesis in science, which is the product of individual imagination but once suggested leads to research that can confirm or disconfirm it. The crucial difference is that the narrative combination of relations is simply not subject to confirmation or disconfirmation, as any one of them taken separately might be. So we have a second dilemma about historical narrative: as historical it claims to represent, through its form, part of the real complexity of the past, but as narrative it is a product of imaginative construction, which cannot defend its claim to truth by any accepted procedure of argument or authentication.

Finally, a third and last question in this budget of paradoxes. In everything I have presented up to this point I have used the terms "event" and "succession of events," and written as if there were no difficulty in distinguishing between a chronicle, or series of statements about events ordered in temporal sequence, and a narrative, which presumably in all cases contains a chronicle but adds to it other forms of ordering, for example causal relations. But hardly any concept is less clear than that of "event." For consider, we may speak of a war as an event, but a war consists of battles, and battles of engagements by units, and engagements by units of actions by individuals; and when the shoe is lost for want of a nail, that is an event too. Now there is no particular difficulty about the concept of a complex event whose parts are themselves events. Uncertainty sets in when we consider the limits of application of the concept. Are there simple or unit-events, that is, events which are not further divisible into events? At the other extreme, what is the maximum complexity and span of time beyond which the application of the term is inappropriate? Is the Renaissance an event? Moreover, it is clear that we cannot refer to events as such, but only to events *under a description;* so there can be more than one description of the same event, all of them true but referring to different aspects of the event or describing it at different levels of generality. But what can we possibly mean by "same event"? Under what description do we refer to the event that is supposed to sustain different descriptions? It seems that the ordinary use of the term "event" presupposes both an already existing division of complex processes into further irreducible elements, and some *standard* description of each putative event; then, to say that there are different descriptions of the "same" event is to say that they are selected from or inferred from that standard and preeminent description.

But in fact we have no idea whether there are minimal or maximal events, and no knowledge of any standard or preeminent descriptions of any events. I am speaking here, of course, of the actual and imaginary events described in the ordinary language of narrative accounts. In the development of natural science, a major function of theory construction and the development of specialized languages has been to establish what *counts* as a unit-event and to provide standard descriptions of events—e.g., the emission of a particle, or one operation of the lever in a Skinner box. In normal science, the uncertainties I have suggested about the concept of event do not arise at all. They are settled by the catechism that every student learns as his induction into the science. But to furnish historiography, or any of our story-telling activities, with an inventory of types of basic events, with standard descriptions of each, could not improve the intelligibility or cognitive value of narratives. This is not because such a project is impossible or undesirable, even if it were both. It is rather because if it were successful it would render narrative form wholly superfluous for the understanding of events; for in stipulating standard descriptions of events (combined with the body of theory that such descriptions are designed to serve) it would rule out the redescriptions that are required in the construction of narrative.

It is not my purpose to create confusion about the concept of "event" but rather to reveal that the confusion has been there all along. Even though we ordinarily think of a narrative as a story about successive and simultaneous events, there is something incompatible about our concept of "event" and our concept of "narrative," which might be put as follows: the concept of event is primarily linked to the conceptual structure of science (and to that part of common sense that has adopted the language and methods of science); but in that conceptual structure it is purged of all narrative connections, and refers to something that can be identified and described without any necessary reference to its location in some process of development—

a process which only narrative form can represent. Therefore, to speak of a "narrative of events" is nearly a contradiction in terms. That it is not perceived as such, I suggest, again reflects the extent to which the idea of Universal History survives as a presupposition. To the extent that historical actuality is regarded as an untold story, then in that untold story our conceptual problems disappear. We can just as well suppose (so long as we do not reflect on it) that it contains the standard descriptions of events to which our descriptions more or less closely approximate, and that it is neatly organized into simple and complex events. Yet all our experience of narratives suggests that there is no way of settling on standard descriptions other than by arbitrary enforcement, and that therefore we cannot without confusion regard different narratives as differently emplotting the "same" events. We need a different way of thinking about narrative. "Events" (or more precisely, descriptions of events) are not the raw material out of which narratives are constructed; rather an event is an abstraction from a narrative. An event may take five seconds or five months, but in either case whether it is one event or many depends not on a definition of "event" but on a particular narrative construction which generates the event's appropriate description. This conception of "event" is not remote from our ordinary responses to stories: in certain stories we can accept even something like the French Revolution as a simple event, because that is the way it is related to characters and plot, while in other stories it may be too complex to describe as a single whole. But if we accept that the description of events is a function of particular narrative structures, we cannot at the same time suppose that the actuality of the past is an untold story. There can in fact be no untold stories at all, just as there can be no unknown knowledge. There can be only past facts not yet described in a context of narrative form.

IV

It should be clear that the three conceptual problems that I have discussed have a common form; they are in fact connected with each other as different ways of bringing out the same conceptual dissonance. All three can best be understood as revealing an incompatibility between our implicit presupposition of what historical narratives are about and our conscious belief that the formal structure of a narrative is constructed rather than discovered. The locus of incompatibility is the presupposition that the structure of a historical narrative, as well as its individual statements taken separately, claims truth as representative of past actuality; so that the past has in its own right a narrative structure which is discovered rather than constructed. It might be worth asking why, if the incompatibility is as sharp as this, it has not been noticed before. One reason, of course, is that it involves a presupposition, and by their very nature presuppositions tend to remain unformulated and therefore uncriticized. A second reason is that very little attention has been paid to the form of historical narratives, as distinguished from the individual statements comprised by that form, as communicating its own unique kind of understanding and explanation. Most often the form of historical narratives has been taken for granted as merely a more or less arbitrary way of setting out the constituent statements which alone make truth-claims. But as we have seen, this cannot be an adequate account of the epistemology of narrative structure in historiography.

When conceptual problems reveal an implicit incompatibility between two concepts, like the present one between the concept of narrative and the concept of historical representation, one may resolve it by expunging either concept. And in fact these conceptual difficulties could be resolved if we could return to the eighteenth-century confidence in Universal History, for which they could not even arise. But such a return is unimaginable. The alternative is to abandon the remnant of the idea of Universal History that survives as a presupposition, namely the idea that there is a determinate historical actuality, the complex referent for all our narratives of "what actually happened," the untold story to which narrative histories approximate. Of course this does not put the past completely at risk; it does not imply that there is nothing determinate about the past, since individual statements of fact, of the sort to which so much historical research is dedicated, remain unaffected. But it does mean that the significance of the past is determinate only by virtue of our own disciplined imagination. Insofar as the significance of past occurrences is understandable only as they are locatable in the ensemble of interrelationships that can be grasped only in the construction of narrative form, it is we who make the past determinate in that respect. If the past is not an untold story but can be made intelligible only as the subject of stories we tell, it is still our responsibility to get on with it.

So narrative history and narrative fiction move closer together than common sense could well accept. Yet the common-sense belief that history is true in a sense in which fiction is not is by no means abrogated, even though what that sense is must be revised. It would be disastrous, I believe, if common sense were to be routed from its last stronghold on this point. For our understanding of fiction needs the contrast with history as much as our understanding of history needs the contrast with fiction. The quality of our responses to imaginative fiction and its uses in our lives require the willing suspension of disbelief; but we could not learn how and when to suspend disbelief except by learning how to distinguish between fiction and history as making different truth-claims for their individual descriptions. If the distinction were to disappear, fiction and history would both collapse back into myth and be indistinguishable from it as from each other. And though myth serves as both fiction and history for those who have not learned to discriminate, we cannot forget what we have learned.

Suggestions for
Further Reading

Discussions of the relationship between literary form and historical understanding occur in works of historiography, literary theory, and philosophy of
history. This volume has attempted to demonstrate the mutual relevance of
work emanating from these fields of scholarship, and the suggestions that
follow are meant to help the reader explore further the work being done in
these several fields. So many items are potentially relevant that any such
guide is necessarily selective, but we have attempted to moderate the effect
of our own biases by incorporating suggestions from our contributors.

Some of the most stimulating discussions of the general issues involved
occur in works primarily devoted to more specific topics. A noteworthy example is Hayden White's *Metahistory: The Historical Imagination in Nineteenth-Century Europe* (Baltimore: Johns Hopkins Univ. Press, 1973). *Metahistory* concentrates on four philosophers—Hegel, Marx, Nietzsche, and
Croce—and four historians—Ranke, Michelet, Tocqueville, and Burckhardt.
As his essay in this volume indicates, White is an intellectual historian who
has been heavily influenced by literary theorists, notably Kenneth Burke,
Northrop Frye, and contemporary structuralists. His conclusions are both
idiosyncratic and controversial; readers interested in nineteenth-century historical thought will want to compare White's book with Maurice Mandelbaum's *History, Man, & Reason: A Study in Nineteenth-Century Thought*
(Baltimore: Johns Hopkins Univ. Press, 1971), and readers interested in the
poetics of history will want to consult many of the other works mentioned
below. But *Metahistory* is clearly a major contribution both to the intellectual
history of its period and to the methodological debate over the literary qualities of historical texts. No one seriously interested in either can afford to
ignore White's book.

Of the figures dealt with in *Metahistory*, Michelet has probably been the
one most often dealt with in ways that recognize the literary dimensions of his
work. Any list of such works would include Roland Barthes, ed., *Michelet
par lui-même* (Paris: Editions du Seuil, 1954); Oscar Haac, *Les Principes
inspirateurs de Michelet* (New Haven: Yale Univ. Press, 1951); the essays of
Michelet in Alain Besançon, *Histoire et expérience du moi* (Paris: Flammar-

151

ion, 1971); and Edmund Wilson, *To the Finland Station* (New York: Harcourt, Brace, 1940); and, perhaps, Stephen Bann, "A Cycle of Historical Discourse: Barante, Thierry, Michelet," *20th Century Studies*, 3 (1970), 110–30. A 1975 Johns Hopkins colloquium on Michelet brought together such historians as White and Besançon and such literary scholars as Haac and Paul Viallaneix; a selection of the papers from this colloquium appeared in *Clio*, Vol. 6, No. 2 (Winter 1977), and the Foreword by guest editor Lionel Gossman cites additional works of interest.

One of the discussants at the Michelet colloquium was David Levin, an Americanist whose *History as Romantic Art* (Stanford: Stanford Univ. Press, 1959) is, like White's book, basic reading for all those interested in history as literature. Levin's volume deals with the nineteenth-century American historians George Bancroft, W. H. Prescott, John Motley, and Francis Parkman, demonstrating the relationship between their historical methods and the literary and intellectual romanticism of the time. Levin is a literary critic with a firm grasp of the historiographical literature and a deep respect for the historian's search for truth; his analysis of the literary qualities of historical writing never threatens to dissolve the distinctions between history and fiction. Also worth reading is a later collection of essays by Levin, *In Defense of Historical Literature* (New York: Hill and Wang, 1967), especially for its lucid opening essay, "The Literary Criticism of History."

Levin's influence is apparent in a work by his student Richard Vitzthum, *The American Compromise: Theme and Method in the Histories of Bancroft, Parkman, and Adams* (Norman: Univ. of Oklahoma Press, 1974). Vitzthum is especially useful as a model for the literary analysis of the way historians make use of their sources. Literary considerations also bulk large in several studies of individual American historians of the nineteenth century. Otis Pease has written an instructive appreciation of Parkman in *Parkman's History: The Historian as a Literary Artist* (New Haven: Yale Univ. Press, 1953). Robert H. Canary's *George Bancroft* (New York: Twayne, 1974) approaches its subject by way of neo-Aristotelian literary criticism and analytic philosophy of history. Melvin Lyon's *Symbol and Idea in Henry Adams* (Lincoln: Univ. of Nebraska Press, 1970) is one of a number of literary studies of Adams.

Literary studies of particular historians have not, of course, been confined to nineteenth-century figures. Another basic work is Leo Braudy's *Narrative Form in History and Fiction: Hume, Fielding, and Gibbon* (Princeton: Princeton Univ. Press, 1970), surely a book of value for anyone interested in the general topic posed by its title. Less sophisticated but still worth reading is J. B. Black, *The Art of History: A Study of Four Great Historians of the Eighteenth Century* (New York: Crofts, 1926), which discusses Voltaire, Hume, Robertson, and Gibbon. Gibbon, whose literary qualities attract both Braudy and Black, has also been the subject of a number of separate studies, notably Harold Bond's *Literary Art of Edward Gibbon* (Oxford: Clarendon, 1960). As Kieran Egan's essay in this volume demonstrates, classicists have long been willing to treat the ancient historians as both historians and literary figures. Egan, of course, takes off from F. M. Cornford's *Thucydides Mythistoricus* (London: Edward Arnald, 1907). Among more recent works we might also mention Frank E. Adcock, *Thucydides and His History* (New York: Cambridge Univ. Press, 1963). Bessie Walker's study *The Annals of Tacitus* (Manchester: Manchester Univ. Press, 1952) is a noteworthy approach to another great classical historian. More general is A. W. Gomme, *The Greek Attitude to Poetry and History* (Berkeley: Univ. of California Press, 1954).

For other historians and periods, we might mention the essays found in two important works: Peter Gay, *Style in History* (New York: Basic Books, 1974), and Arnaldo Momigliano, *Studies in Historiography* (New York: Harper & Row, 1966). Less sensitive to aesthetic considerations but insightful nevertheless is Pieter Geyl in *Encounters in History* (New York: Meridian, 1961). Also rather more ideological than literary in interest is Georg Iggers, *The German Conception of History: The National Tradition of Historical Thought from Herder to the Present* (Middletown, Conn.: Wesleyan Univ. Press, 1968), which is fundamental reading even so. Literature, or at least rhetoric, is more central to Nancy S. Struever's *Language of History in the Renaissance: Rhetoric and Historical Consciousness in Florentine Humanism* (Princeton: Princeton Univ. Press, 1970); readers unfamiliar with the humanists might prefer to encounter Struever's methodological position in her essay "The Study of Language and the Study of History," *Journal of Interdisciplinary History*, 4 (1974), 401–15. Issues like those in Struever's volume are also discussed in Donald R. Kelley's *Foundations of Modern Historical Scholarship: Language, Law and History in the French Renaissance* (New York: Columbia Univ. Press, 1970). A later period in French historiography is covered by Boris Reizov, *L'Historiographie romantique française* (Moscow: Editions en langues étranges, 1956). And twentieth-century American historians are the focus of Gene Wise's *American Historical Explanations* (Homewood, Ill.: Dorsey, 1973). Wise, like scholars in many fields of intellectual history, has been much influenced by Thomas Kuhn's *The Structure of Scientific Revolutions* (Chicago: Univ. of Chicago Press, 1962), and his "explanation-forms" are openly derived from Kuhn's "paradigms." Although concerned with literary matters only in passing, Wise's book is, among other things, excellent background reading for the Richard Reinitz essay in this volume. It may well be that the most promising approach for future historiography lies in some combination of Wise's "explanation-forms" with the kind of formal literary analysis advocated by Hayden White.

Historians who do not specialize in historiography most often turn their attention to literary matters when considering literary works as source material for history or when advising the younger historian to write well. It seems to some that this century's advances in professionalism and objectivity have been balanced by a decline in literary skill. That this is not a recent attitude only is shown by the title essay of Philip Guedella's book *The Missing Muse* (New York: Harper, 1930). Exhortations to improve the quality of historical writing are sometimes placed in the context of a defense of traditional narrative history and the notion of history as an art rather than a science. These aspects are present in Allan Nevins and Catherine Drinker Bowen, *The Art of History* (Washington: U. S. Government Printing Office, 1967); Leslie Byrd Simpson, *The Writing of History: A Dialogue* (Berkeley: Univ. of California Press, 1947); Arthur Bryant, *The Art of Writing History* (Oxford: Oxford Univ. Press, 1946). Literary form is, however, a matter of concern to all sorts of historians, as is demonstrated by Brian Stock, "Literary Discourse and the Social Historian," *New Literary History,* 8 (1977), 183–94. Robert F. Berkhofer, Jr., *A Behavioral Approach to Historical Analysis* (New York: Free Press, 1969), commends itself as an antidote to the more violent attacks on behavioral history—and as an example that one may write about such matters in good prose. H. Stuart Hughes, *History as Art and as Science* (New York: Harper & Row, 1964) examines both sides. Other relevant works are I. E. Cadenhead, Jr., ed., *Literature and History* (Tulsa: Univ. of Tulsa Press, 1970); Walter Laqueur, "Literature and the Historian," *Journal of Contemporary History,* 2 (1967), 5–14; Robert H. Bremmer, ed., *Essays on History and Literature* (Columbus: Ohio State Univ. Press, 1966); A. R. Louch, "History as Narrative," *History and Theory,* 8 (1969), 54–70; Emery Neff, *The Poetry of History* (New York: Columbia Univ. Press, 1947).

The question of whether history as a branch of knowledge is an art or a science is a philosophical one, if it is a meaningful question at all, and one can find more sophisticated (albeit more abstract) discussions of this question in philosophical literature. Most of the contributors to this volume have been influenced to some degree by those who hold that narrative accounts may in fact constitute a kind of explanation different from that employed in the physical sciences, and, of course, Louis Mink's essay examines the question of the meaningfulness of narrative. For a useful survey of the varieties of the "narrativist" position, see W. H. Dray, "On the Nature and Role of Narrative in Historiography," *History and Theory,* 10 (1971), 153–71. Other items worth noting are Louis O. Mink, "History and Fiction as Modes of Comprehension," *New Literary History,* 1 (1970), 541–58; W. B. Gallie, *Philosophy and the Historical Understanding* (New York: Schocken, 1968); and W. H. Walsh, " 'Plain' and 'Significant' Narrative in History," *Journal of Philosophy,* 65 (1958), 479–84.

Several of those inclined to take narrative explanation seriously have been influenced by R. G. Collingwood's posthumous book, *The Idea of History* (Oxford: Clarendon, 1946; rpt. New York: Oxford Univ. Press, 1956). Collingwood, perhaps because he was a historian as well as a philosopher, is also better known to historians than most philosophers of history. A literary critic, Donald S. Taylor, is engaged in an effort to wed Collingwood's thought to the literary theories of R. S. Crane; see his "R. G. Collingwood: Art, Craft, and History," *Clio,* 2 (1973), 263–78, and "Literary Criticism and Historical Inference," *Clio,* 5 (1976), 345–70. For a sympathetic defense of Collingwood's position, see Louis O. Mink, *Mind, History, and Dialectic: The Philosophy of R. G. Collingwood* (Bloomington: Indiana Univ. Press, 1969). Also relevant are some of the essays in Michael Krausz, ed., *Critical Essays on the Philosophy of R. G. Collingwood* (Oxford: Clarendon, 1972).

Credit for focusing the attention of philosophy of history on the question of explanation, however, goes not to Collingwood but to Carl G. Hempel, "The Function of General Laws in History," *Journal of Philosophy,* 39 (1942), 35–48. In attempting to assimilate historical explanation to a more general model of explanation, Hempel set off a long-running debate. Like the historians' debate over whether history is an art or a science, the debate over the nature of historical explanation reflected basic epistemological positions. A number of collections include key essays on this question, among them W. H. Dray, ed., *Philosophical Analysis and History* (New York: Harper & Row, 1966); Patrick Gardiner, ed., *Theories of History* (New York: Free Press, 1959); and Sidney Hook, ed., *Philosophy and History* (New York: New York Univ. Press, 1963). Most studies in the critical philosophy of history have been touched by this debate, and we can take time only to cite those whose discussion of explanation seems to us to have cast light on historical narratives as literary works: Arthur C. Danto, *Analytical Philosophy of History* (Cambridge: Cambridge Univ. Press, 1956); W. H. Dray, *Laws and Explanation in History* (New York: Oxford Univ. Press, 1957); Haskell Fain, *Between Philosophy and History* (Princeton: Princeton Univ. Press, 1970); C. B. McCullagh, "Narrative and Explanation in History," *Mind,* 78 (1969), 256–61; Maurice Mandelbaum, "A Note on History as Narrative," *History and Theory,* 6 (1967), 414–19, and the replies to it by Richard Ely, W. H. Dray, and Rolf Gruner in *History and Theory,* 8 (1969), 275–94; Louis O. Mink, "Philosophical Analysis and Historical Understanding," *Review of Metaphysics,* 21 (1968), 667–98; Peter Munz, "The Skeleton and the Mollusc: Reflections on the Nature of Historical Narratives," *New Zealand Journal of History,* 1 (1967), 107–23; Maurice Natanson, *Literature, Philosophy and the Social Sciences* (The Hague: Nijhoff, 1962); N. M. L. Nathan, "History, Literature, and the Classification of Knowledge," *The Australasian Journal of Philosophy,* 48 (1970), 213–33; Frederick A. Olafson, "Narrative History and the Concept of Action," *History and Theory,* 9 (1970), 265–89; and Morton White, *Foundations of Historical Knowledge* (New York: Harper & Row, 1965).

The list just given doubtless omits some items that readers would find instructive on the matters dealt with in this volume. For our purposes, in any case, it may well matter less whether narrative is a distinctive kind of explanation than that the controversy has led a number of philosophers to examine rigorously the nature of historical narratives. Although the question of historical explanation may be taking new directions, such useful fallout continues, as in recent essays by Teun A. van Dijk, "Action, Action Description, and Narrative," *New Literary History,* 6 (1975), 273–94, and David L. Hull, "Central Subjects and Historical Narratives," *History and Theory,* 14 (1975),

253–74. Maurice Mandelbaum, who made an early contribution to the discussion with *The Problem of Historical Knowledge* (New York: Liveright, 1938), has recently published *The Anatomy of Historical Knowledge* (Baltimore: Johns Hopkins Univ. Press, 1977). Among other things, Mandelbaum points out that not all historical works assume the form of sequential narratives. One can welcome the fact that some philosophers are turning their attention to histories organized in other ways; such histories also have literary forms and qualities whose nature we may be helped to understand by the sort of analysis to which narrative history has been subjected.

Although philosophers may, in general, be better equipped than historians for rigorous argument about the proper place of history in our structure of knowledge, we can hardly ignore the comments of historians upon their own craft. Non-historians particularly need to immerse themselves in such accounts before venturing to discuss the literary form taken by a piece of historical research in its final incarnation. To understand the process that precedes the writing, one can examine the generally frank and personal accounts in L. P. Curtis, Jr., ed., *The Historian's Workshop* (New York: Knopf, 1970), or more methodologically oriented collections such as Fritz Stern, ed., *Varieties of History* (New York: Meridian, 1956), or A. S. Eisenstadt, ed., *The Craft of American History* (New York: Harper & Row, 1966). Among other useful works are Philippe Ariès, *Le Temps de l'histoire* (Monaco: Editions du Rocher, 1956); Carl Becker, *Everyman His Own Historian* (New York: Appleton-Century-Crofts, 1935); Marc L. Bloch, *The Historian's Craft,* trans. Peter Putnam (New York: Knopf, 1953); Fernand Braudel, *Ecrits sur l'histoire* (Paris: Flammarion, 1969); Herbert Butterfield, ''Narrative History and the Spade-Work Behind It,'' *History,* 52 (1968), 165–80; E. H. Carr, *What Is History?* (New York: Knopf, 1962); J. H. Hexter, *The History Primer* (New York: Basic Books, 1971); Chaim Perelman, *Les Catégories en histoire* (Brussels: Université libre de Bruxelles, 1969), and *Raisonnement et démarches de l'historien* (Brussels: Université libre de Bruxelles, 1963); Page Smith, *The Historian and History* (New York: Knopf, 1964); and Paul Veyne, *Comment on écrit l'histoire: Essai d'épistémologie* (Paris: Editions du Seuil, 1971).

Recorded history is, of course, a mere fraction of mankind's life on this earth, and living in the linear time of history is a very different thing from living in the cyclic time of the seasons and myth. The appeal to myth in the essays by Hayden White and Kieran Egan in this volume may even suggest to some that historical writing is our way of accommodating to change by bottling it in changeless story-forms. For more on history and myth, see Ernst Cassirer, *An Essay on Man* (New Haven: Yale Univ. Press, 1944); Mircea Eliade, *The Myth of the Eternal Return,* trans. Willard Trask (New York: Pantheon, 1954), later printed as *Cosmos and History* (New York: Harper & Row, 1959); Peter Munz, ''History and Myth,'' *Philosophical Quarterly,* 6 (1956), 1–17; and Alfred Stern, ''Fiction and Myth in History,'' *Diogenes,* No. 42 (Summer 1963), 98–118. For a speculative account of man's developing historical sense, see Stephen Toulmin and June Goodfriend, *The Discovery of Time* (New York: Harper & Row, 1965). The Toulmin and Goodfriend book might well be read alongside Jerome H. Buckley's *Triumph of Time: A Study of the Victorian Concepts of Time, History, Progress, and Decadence* (Cambridge, Mass.: Harvard Univ. Press, 1966), or Emile Benveniste's essay "La Relation de temps dans le verbe française" in his *Problèmes de linguistique générale* (Paris: Gallimard, 1966). For a useful survey of notions of myth, see G. S. Kirk, *The Nature of Greek Myths* (Harmondsworth, Middlesex: Penguin Books, 1974). Most American critics who apply the notion of "myth" to narrative structures have been influenced by Northrop Frye's *Anatomy of Criticism: Four Essays* (Princeton: Princeton Univ. Press, 1957).

For general discussions of narrative structure, see Robert Scholes and Robert Kellogg, *The Nature of Narrative* (New York: Oxford Univ. Press, 1966); Harold Toliver, *Animate Illusions: Explanations of Narrative Structure* (Lincoln: Univ. of Nebraska Press, 1974); Warner Berthoff, *Fictions and Events* (New York: Dutton, 1971); Frank Kermode, *The Sense of an Ending* (Oxford: Oxford Univ. Press, 1967); Ronald Barthes, "An Introduction to the Structural Analysis of Narrative," trans. Lionel Dusuit, *New Literary History*, 6 (1975), 237–72; Seymour Chatman, "New Ways of Analyzing Narrative Structure," *Language and Style*, 2 (1969), 1–36, and "Towards a Theory of Narrative," *New Literary History*, 6 (1975), 295–318; essays collected in Roger Fowler, ed., *Style and Structure in Literature* (Ithaca: Cornell Univ. Press, 1975); A. J. Greimas and J. Courtés, "The Cognitive Dimension of Narrative Discourse," trans. Michael Rengstorf, *New Literary History*, 7 (1976), 433–47; Paul Ricoeur, "The Model of the Text: Meaningful Action Considered as a Text," *New Literary History*, 5 (1973), 91–117; and John R. Searle, "The Logical Status of Fictional Discourse," *New Literary History*, 6 (1975), 319–32. Particularly relevant are two recent essays by Paul Hernadi, "Clio's Cousins: Historiography Considered as Translation, Fiction, and Criticism," *New Literary History*, 7 (1976), 247–57, and "Re-Presenting the Past: A Note on Narrative Historiography and Historical Drama," *History and Theory*, 15 (1976), 45–51. There is much that is relevant to historical writing in general in Georg Lukacs, *The Historical Novel*, trans. Hannah and Stanley Mitchell (Boston: Beacon, 1963). Erich Auerbach, *Mimesis*, trans. Willard Trask (Princeton: Princeton Univ. Press, 1953) is often suggestive. Among the many relevant works of Kenneth Burke, we would especially like to see more attention paid to his *Attitudes toward History* (New York: The New Republic, 1937). There are some materials of interest in two collections of English Institute essays: Phillip Damon, ed., *Literary Criticism and Historical Understanding* (New York: Columbia Univ. Press, 1967); and Angus Fletcher, ed., *The Literature of Fact* (New York: Columbia Univ. Press, 1976).

Most of the books and articles cited above will lead the reader to yet other books and articles of interest and use. For more recent material, the reader interested in pursuing the question of literary form and historical understanding should consult the standard bibliographies in the various relevant fields. For historiography, there is a fairly recent annotated bibliography in Lester D. Stephens, ed., *Historiography* (Metuchen, N.J.: Scarecrow Press, 1975). *History and Theory* is the leading journal for philosophy of history and historiography. *Clio: An Interdisciplinary Journal of Literature, History, and the Philosophy of History* is especially interested in the literary analysis of historical writings, and a new English journal, *Literature and History,* shares this interest. Among more purely literary journals, *New Literary History* has published a number of articles on history as literature and the theory of narrative. Much of the best work on our topic is relatively recent; no doubt there is much left to be done, and we hope that this volume will help stimulate such studies.

INDEX